Welcome!

We value your
and hope you enjo'
Munro Hiking Journal & Log Book.

GW00499487

Name _____

_____

Contact _____

contact us at xpanama@mail.com

CONTENTS

- Welcome & Easy Guide
- Calendar Planning Section
- Munro Lists & Bucket Lists
- Map of Scotland
- Milestone Records
- Personal Programme (M) or (P)
- Countdown Chart
- Club Information
- Essential Kit
- Hiking Checklists
- Events Record Sheets
  +++ 284 Activity Pages (2 spare!) +++
- Notes & Drawing Pages

EASY GUIDE

Circle or annotate <u>all or as many icons as you wish</u>
Use a bright shade of pen e.g. red or blue so it stands out.
Use notes section to add detail where required.
Enjoy and good luck with your Hiking!

 MAGAZINE/ GUIDE BOOK PROGRAMME

 OWN PERSONAL PROGRAMME

 You can log whether you have a heavy or light loading / rucksack (User Defined)

My Ref Create your own Reference system for Drawings/ Camera Settings etc

 Specify which set of Shoes or Boots you are using. Handy when using/trying new kit

sunny
cloudy
rain
snow
windy

TEMP
E.g.
Hot /
Mild /
Cold

THE PLAN

Date

Meet up time/ location

Est. Duration

Est. Distance   Km
                       Miles

Local Contact

MUNRO NAME

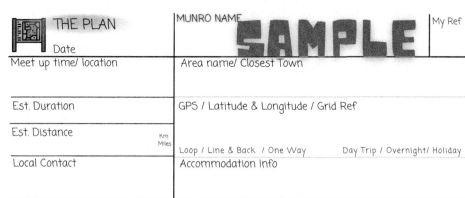

SAMPLE

My Ref

Area name/ Closest Town

GPS / Latitude & Longitude / Grid Ref

Loop / Line & Back / One Way   Day Trip / Overnight/ Holiday

Accommodation Info

THE EQUIPMENT

A   B

Map Name/No

THE HIKE

(M)   (P)

Start Time

End Time

Actual Distance

Total No of Steps

Calories
Burned

POINTS OF INTEREST

Difficulty Level (1 Easy 5 Hard) △

Enjoyment Level (1 Bad 5 Good) ♡

Overall Grade (1 Bad 5 Good) ☆

Notes
Facilities
Parking
Costs
Nature
Etc

284 ENTRY SHEETS IN THIS BOOK (2 SPARE!)

MY MUNRO TOTAL

	JAN	FEB	MAR	APR	MAY	JUN	
1							1
2							2
3							3
4							4
5							5
6							6
7							7
8							8
9							9
10							10
11							11
12							12
13							13
14							14
15							15
16							16
17							17
18							18
19							19
20							20
21							21
22							22
23							23
24							24
25							25
26							26
27							27
28							28
29							29
30							30
31							31

	JUL	AUG	SEP	OCT	NOV	DEC	
1							1
2							2
3							3
4							4
5							5
6							6
7							7
8							8
9							9
10							10
11							11
12							12
13							13
14							14
15							15
16							16
17							17
18							18
19							19
20							20
21							21
22							22
23							23
24							24
25							25
26							26
27							27
28							28
29							29
30							30
31							31

PERSONAL PROGRAMME NOTES

Your hike may be part of a specific programme, for example a Magazine or Guide Book Challenge
(denoted by this symbol (M) on your record sheets)
or it may be another programme or event such as your
'Summer Holidays Challenge' where you are walking 20 trails or 100 miles etc
(denoted by (P) on the record sheets).
Use these pages to set out what your programme is. Enjoy the journey!

"There are no shortcuts to any place worth going." - Beverly Sills

"Don't Fear moving slowly Forward...Fear standing still."
— Kathleen Harris

BUCKET LIST

Goals

_____
_____
_____
_____
_____
_____
_____
_____
_____

To-Do List

_____
_____
_____
_____
_____
_____
_____
_____

Notes

_____
_____
_____
_____
_____
_____
_____

"It's not the mountain we conquer, but ourselves." - Sir Edmund Hillary

"Get going ... walk if you have to. but finish the damned race." — Ron Hill

In the following pages Munros are grouped
in their specific geographical areas.
Each area has the peaks listed in descending order.

Page	Area
1a	Loch Ericht / Loch Linnhe
1b	Loch Broom / Cape Wrath
2a	Loch Maree / Loch Broom
2b	The Scottish Islands
3a	Loch Fyne / Loch Tay
3b	Glen Roy / Monadh Liath
3c	Loch Broom / Cromarty Firth
4a	Loch Tay / Rannoch Moor
4b	Loch Ericht / Drumochter
5a	Glen Orchy / Loch Leven
5b	Glen Carron / Glen Torridon
6a	Glen Shee / Mount Keen
6b	Glen Affric / Glen Shiel
7a	Drumochter / Glen Shee
7b	The Cairngorms
8a	Loch Eil / Glen Shiel
8b	Glen Cannich / Glen Carron

1a		Loch Ericht / Loch Linnhe		
✓	Date	Munro	Altitude	
			feet	metres
		Ben Nevis	4409	1344
		Aonach Beag (Glen Nevis)	4049	1234
		Aonach Mor	4006	1221
		Carn Mor Dearg	4003	1220
		Stob Choire Claurigh	3862	1177
		Ben Alder	3766	1148
		Geal-Charn (Alder)	3714	1132
		Binnein Mor	3707	1130
		Aonach Beag (Alder)	3661	1116
		Stob Coire an Laoigh	3661	1116
		Stob Coire Easain (Loch Treig)	3658	1115
		Stob a' Choire Mheadhoin	3625	1105
		Beinn Eibhinn	3615	1102
		Sgurr a' Mhaim	3606	1099
		Sgurr Choinnich Mor	3589	1094
		Beinn a' Chlachair	3566	1087
		Na Gruagaichean	3465	1056
		Geal Charn (Laggan)	3442	1049
		Chno Dearg	3432	1046
		Carn Dearg (Alder)	3392	1034
		Am Bodach (Mamores)	3386	1032
		Beinn Bheoil	3343	1019
		Sgurr Eilde Mor	3314	1010
		Stob Ban (Mamores)	3278	999
		An Gearanach	3222	982
		Stob Coire a' Chairn	3219	981
		Stob Coire Sgriodain	3212	979
		Stob Ban (Grey Corries)	3205	977
		Sgor Gaibhre	3133	955
		Binnein Beag	3094	943
		Carn Dearg (Corrour)	3087	941
		Mullach nan Coirean	3081	939
		Beinn na Lap	3068	935
		Creag Pitridh	3031	924

1b		Loch Broom / Cape Wrath		
✓	Date	Munro	Altitude	
			feet	metres
		Ben More Assynt	3274	998
		Conival	3238	987
		Meall nan Con (Ben Klibreck)	3156	962
		Ben Hope	3041	927

2a		Loch Maree / Loch Broom		
✓	Date	Munro	Altitude	
			feet	metres
		Sgurr Mor (Fannaichs)	3635	1110
		Sgurr nan Clach Geala	3586	1093
		Bidein a' Ghlas Thuill (An Teallach)	3484	1062
		Sgurr Fiona (An Teallach)	3478	1060
		Mullach Coire Mhic Fhearchair	3343	1018
		Sgurr Breac	3278	999
		A' Chailleach (Fannaichs)	3271	997
		Sgurr Ban (Fisherfield)	3245	989
		Slioch	3219	981
		A' Mhaighdean	3173	967
		Beinn Liath Mhor Fannaich	3130	954
		Meall Gorm	3114	949
		Beinn Tarsuinn	3074	937
		Meall a' Chrasgaidh	3064	934
		Fionn Bheinn	3061	933
		An Coileachan	3028	923
		Sgurr nan Each	3028	923
		Ruadh Stac Mor	3012	918

2b		The Scottish Islands		
✓	Date	Munro	Altitude	
			feet	metres
		Sgurr Alasdair	3255	992
		Sgurr Dearg (Inaccessible point)	3235	986
		Sgurr a' Ghreadaidh	3189	973
		Ben More (Mull)	3169	966
		Sgurr na Banachdich	3166	965
		Sgurr nan Gillean	3163	964
		Bruach na Frithe	3143	958
		Sgurr Mhic Choinnich	3110	948
		Sgurr Dubh Mor	3097	944
		Am Basteir	3064	934
		Bla Bheinn	3045	928
		Sgurr nan Eag	3031	924
		Sgurr a' Mhadaidh	3012	918

3a		Loch Fyne to Loch Tay		
✓	Date	Munro	Altitude	
			feet	metres
		Ben More (Crianlarich)	3852	1174
		Stob Binnein	3822	1165
		Ben Lui	3707	1130
		Cruach Ardrain	3432	1046
		Ben Oss	3376	1029
		Beinn Ime	3317	1011
		An Caisteal	3264	995
		Ben Vorlich (Loch Earn)	3232	985
		Beinn Dubhchraig	3209	978
		Stuc a' Chroin	3199	975
		Ben Lomond	3196	974
		Beinn Bhuidhe	3110	948
		Beinn Tulaichean	3104	946
		Ben Vorlich (Arrochar)	3094	943
		Beinn a' Chroin	3084	940
		Beinn Chabhair	3061	933
		Ben Chonzie	3054	931
		Beinn Narnain	3041	926
		Beinn a' Chleibh	3005	916
		Ben Vane	3004	916

3b		Monadh Liath / Glen Roy		
✓	Date	Munro	Altitude	
			feet	metres
		Creag Meagaidh	3701	1128
		Stob Poite Coire Ardair	3458	1054
		Beinn a' Chaorainn (Laggan)	3451	1049
		Carn Liath (Meagaidh)	3301	1006
		Carn Dearg (Monadh Liath)	3100	945
		A' Chailleach (Monadh Liath)	3051	930
		Geal Charn (Monadh Liath)	3038	926
		Carn Sgulain	3018	920
		Beinn Teallach	3001	915

3c		Loch Broom / Cromarty Firth		
✓	Date	Munro	Altitude	
			feet	metres
		Beinn Dearg (Ullapool)	3556	1084
		Glas Leathad Mor (Ben Wyvis)	3432	1046
		Cona' Mheall	3209	978
		Meall nan Ceapraichean	3205	977
		Am Faochagach	3127	953
		Eididh nan Clach Geala	3041	927
		Seana Bhraigh	3038	926

4a			Rannoch Moor / Loch Tay		
✔	Date		Munro	feet	metres
			Ben Lawers	3983	1214
			An Stuc	3668	1118
			Meall Garbh (Lawers)	3668	1118
			Beinn Ghlas	3619	1103
			Schiehallion	3553	1083
			Beinn a' Chreachain	3547	1081
			Beinn Heasgarnich	3537	1078
			Beinn Dorain	3530	1076
			Meall Corranaich	3507	1069
			Creag Mhor	3435	1047
			Meall nan Tarmachan	3425	1044
			Carn Mairg	3415	1041
			Meall Ghaordaidh	3409	1039
			Beinn Achaladair	3406	1038
			Carn Gorm	3376	1029
			Ben Challum	3363	1025
			Beinn an Dothaidh	3294	1004
			Meall Greigh	3284	1001
			Meall na Aighean	3219	981
			Meall Garbh (Glen Lyon)	3176	968
			Stuchd an Lochain	3150	960
			Meall Glas	3146	959
			Beinn Mhanach	3127	953
			Meall Buidhe	3058	932
			Meall a' Choire Leith	3038	926
			Sgiath Chuil	3022	921

4b			Loch Ericht / Drumochter		
✔	Date		Munro	feet	metres
			Beinn Udlamain	3317	1011
			Sgairneach Mhor	3251	991
			A' Mharconaich	3199	975
			Meall Chuaich	3120	951
			Carn na Caim	3087	941
			A' Bhuidheanach Bheag	3071	936
			Geal-charn	3009	917

5a		Glen Orchy / Loch Leven		
✓	Date	Munro	Altitude feet	metres
		Bidean nam Bian	3773	1150
		Ben Cruachan	3694	1126
		Meall a' Bhuiridh	3635	1108
		Creise	3609	1100
		Stob Ghabhar	3576	1090
		Ben Starav	3537	1078
		Stob Coire Sgreamhach	3517	1072
		Stob Coir' an Albannaich	3425	1044
		Sgorr Dhearg (Beinn a' Bheithir)	3360	1024
		Stob Dearg (Buchaille Etive Mor)	3353	1021
		Sgorr Dhonuill (Beinn a' Bheithir)	3284	1001
		Stob Diamh	3274	998
		Glas Bheinn Mhor	3271	997
		Sgor na h-Ulaidh	3261	994
		Beinn Eunaich	3245	989
		Beinn a' Chochuill	3215	980
		Sgorr nam Fiannaidh (Aonach Eagach)	3173	967
		Beinn nan Aighenan	3150	960
		Beinn Fhionnlaidh (Appin)	3146	959
		Stob Dubh (Buchaille Etive Beag)	3143	958
		Stob na Broige	3136	956
		Meall Dearg (Aonach Eagach)	3127	953
		Stob a' Choire Odhair	3100	945
		Beinn Sgulaird	3074	937
		Meall nan Eun	3045	928
		Stob Coire Raineach	3035	925

5b		Glen Carron / Glen Torridon		
✓	Date	Munro	Altitude feet	metres
		Spidean a' Choire Leith (Liathach)	1055	3461
		Mullach an Rathain (Liathach)	1023	3356
		Ruadh-stac Mor (Beinn Eighe)	1010	3314
		Spidean Coire nan Clach (Beinn Eighe)	993	3258
		Sgurr Mhor (Beinn Alligin)	986	3235
		Sgorr Ruadh	962	3156
		Maol Chean-dearg (Torridon)	933	3061
		Beinn Liath Mhor (Achnashellach)	926	3038
		Tom na Gruagaich (Beinn Alligin)	922	3025

6a		Glen Shee / Mount Keen		
✔	Date	Munro	Altitude	
			feet	metres
		Cac Carn Beag (Lochnagar)	3789	1155
		Carn a' Choire Bhoidheach	3642	1110
		Glas Maol	3504	1068
		Cairn of Claise	3491	1064
		Carn an t-Sagairt Mor	3435	1047
		Carn an Tuirc	3343	1019
		Cairn Bannoch	3320	1012
		Broad Cairn	3274	998
		Creag Leacach	3238	987
		Tolmount	3143	958
		Tom Buidhe	3140	957
		Driesh	3107	947
		Mount Keen	3081	939
		Mayar	3045	928

6b		Glen Affric / Glen Shiel		
✔	Date	Munro	Altitude	
			feet	metres
		Carn Eige	3881	1183
		Mam Sodhail	3875	1181
		Sgurr nan Ceathreamhnan	3776	1151
		A' Chralaig	3675	1120
		Tom a' Choinich	3648	1112
		Sgurr nan Conbhairean	3638	1109
		Mullach Fraoch-choire	3615	1102
		Sgurr Fhuaran	3501	1067
		Toll Creagach	3458	1054
		Sgurr a' Bhealaich Dheirg	3399	1036
		Beinn Fhada (Kintail)	3386	1032
		Sgurr na Ciste Duibhe	3369	1027
		Beinn Fhionnlaidh (Affric)	3297	1005
		Sail Chaorainn	3287	1002
		Sgurr na Carnach	3287	1002
		Aonach Meadhoin	3284	1001
		Mullach na Dheiragain	3222	982
		Ciste Dhubh	3212	979
		Carn Ghluasaid	3140	957
		Saileag	3136	956
		An Socach (Glen Affric)	3022	921
		A' Ghlas-bheinn	3012	918

7a		Drumochter / Glen Shee		
✓	Date	Munro	Altitude	
			feet	metres
		Carn nan Gabhar (Beinn a' Ghlo)	3678	1121
		Braigh Coire Chruinn-bhalgain	3510	1070
		Glas Tulaichean	3448	1051
		Beinn Iutharn Mhor	3428	1045
		Carn an Righ	3376	1029
		Beinn Dearg (Atholl)	3307	1008
		An Sgarsoch	3301	1006
		Carn an Fhidhleir (Carn Ealar)	3261	994
		Carn a' Gheoidh	3199	975
		Carn Liath (Beinn a'Ghlo)	3199	975
		Carn a' Chlamain	3159	963
		Carn Bhac	3104	946
		An Socach (Glen Ey)	3097	944
		The Cairnwell	3061	933
		Carn Aosda	3009	917

7b		The Cairngorms		
✓	Date	Munro	Altitude	
			feet	metres
		Ben Macdui	4295	1309
		Braeriach	4252	1296
		Cairn Toul	4236	1291
		Sgor an Lochain Uaine	4127	1258
		Cairn Gorm	4081	1244
		Beinn a' Bhuird North Top	3927	1197
		Beinn Mheadhoin	3878	1182
		Leabaidh an Daimh Bhuidhe (Ben Avon)	3842	1171
		Beinn Bhrotain	3796	1157
		Derry Cairngorm	3789	1155
		Sgor Gaoith	3668	1118
		Monadh Mor	3652	1113
		Bynack More	3576	1090
		Beinn a' Chaorainn (Glen Derry)	3550	1083
		Carn a' Mhaim	3402	1037
		Mullach Clach a' Bhlair	3343	1019
		The Devil's Point	3294	1004
		Beinn Bhreac	3054	931

8a		Loch Eil /Glen Shiel		
✓	Date	Munro	Altitude	
			feet	metres
		Sgurr na Ciche	3412	1040
		Gleouraich	3396	1035
		Sgurr a' Mhaoraich	3369	1027
		Aonach air Chrith	3350	1021
		Ladhar Bheinn	3346	1020
		Garbh Chioch Mhor	3323	1013
		The Saddle	3314	1010
		Sgurr an Doire Leathain	3314	1010
		Sgurr an Lochain	3294	1004
		Sgurr Mor	3291	1003
		Spidean Mialach	3268	996
		Druim Shionnach	3238	987
		Gulvain	3238	987
		Maol Chinn-dearg (Glen Shiel)	3219	981
		Beinn Sgritheall	3196	974
		Sgurr Thuilm	3159	963
		Sgurr nan Coireachan (Glen Finnan)	3136	956
		Sgurr nan Coireachan	3127	953
		Creag a' Mhaim	3107	947
		Meall Buidhe (Knoydart)	3104	946
		Sgurr na Sgine	3104	946
		Luinne Bheinn	3081	939
		Sron a' Choire Ghairbh	3074	937
		Gairich	3015	919
		Creag nan Damh	3012	918
		Meall na Teanga	3012	918

8b		Glen Cannich / Glen Carron		
✓	Date	Munro	Altitude	
			feet	metres
		Sgurr na Lapaich (Glen Cannich)	3773	1150
		An Riabhachan	3704	1129
		Sgurr a' Choire Ghlais	3553	1083
		An Socach (Glen Cannich)	3507	1069
		Sgurr a' Chaorachain (Monar)	3455	1053
		Sgurr Fhuar-thuill	3442	1049
		Maoile Lunndaidh	3304	1007
		Sgurr Choinnich	3278	999
		Sgurr na Ruaidhe	3258	993
		Carn nan Gobhar (Glen Cannich)	3255	992
		Carn nan Gobhar (Glen Strathfarrar)	3255	992
		Lurg Mhor	3235	986
		Bidein a' Choire Sheasgaich	3100	945
		Moruisg	3045	928

Milestone Record

Use this to log key areas that interest you to show progression over the whole programme
E.g. Distance Covered In A Season or Number of Tors etc

Area	Date							

Area	Date							

Milestone Record

Use this to log key areas that interest you to show progression over the whole programme
E.g. Distance Covered In A Season or Number of Tors etc

Area	Date

Area	Date

Countdown Chart

Use this table for example a major hike coming up or training for an event
- or just a 12 week planner / countdown. Plan ahead. Enjoy the journey!

Weeks to go		Notes	Complete
12			
11			
10			
9			
8			
7			
6			
5			
4			
3			
2			
1			

WALKING/HIKING CLUB

Club/Group Name	
Address	
Key Contact	
Telephone Number	
Email	

Meeting Days	
Meeting Times	
Other Information	

Routes / Events / Personal Times etc

"After a day's walk, everything has twice its usual value." - G.M. Trevelyan

MY EVENTS / MEETINGS

Plan ahead. Enjoy the journey!

DATE	Event	Distance	Actual Time	Position

Notes

DATE	Event	Distance	Actual Time	Position

Notes

DATE	Event	Distance	Actual Time	Position

Notes

DATE	Event	Distance	Actual Time	Position

Notes

DATE	Event	Distance	Actual Time	Position

Notes

DATE	Event	Distance	Actual Time	Position

Notes

MY EVENTS / MEETINGS

Plan ahead. Enjoy the journey!

DATE	Event	Distance	Actual Time	Position

Notes

DATE	Event	Distance	Actual Time	Position

Notes

DATE	Event	Distance	Actual Time	Position

Notes

DATE	Event	Distance	Actual Time	Position

Notes

DATE	Event	Distance	Actual Time	Position

Notes

DATE	Event	Distance	Actual Time	Position

Notes

MY EVENTS / MEETINGS

Plan ahead. Enjoy the journey!

DATE	Event	Distance	Actual Time	Position

Notes

DATE	Event	Distance	Actual Time	Position

Notes

DATE	Event	Distance	Actual Time	Position

Notes

DATE	Event	Distance	Actual Time	Position

Notes

DATE	Event	Distance	Actual Time	Position

Notes

DATE	Event	Distance	Actual Time	Position

Notes

"When everything feels like an uphill struggle. Just think of the view from the top." - Anonymous

ESSENTIAL KIT

This of course is dependant on the remoteness and difficulty of your hike.
But it is always useful to remind yourself and to stay safe.

1 Map & Compass, Pen Knife ☐

2 Walking Shoes / Boots & spare Dry socks ☐

3 Enough Food & Water ☐

4 (Reserve) Waterproof Clothing & Warm Hat ☐

5 First Aid Kit / Basic Repair Kit ☐

6 Sunscreen, Sun Glasses ☐

7 Fully Charged Mobile Phone / Battery Reserve ☐

8 Torch & Matches/ Lighter ☐

9 Camera Equipt, Battery solutions ☐

10 This Journal & Pen ☐

WALKING / HIKING PLAN

Event / Route   Date

1 Choose Location & Route (Check Reviews) ☐

2 Research Conditions, Weather etc ☐

3 Plan Route, Stops & Timings ☐

4 Travel Planning:How to get there & back ☐

5 Check RainFall, Sunrise & Sunset Times ☐

6 Research terrain - correct footwear ☐

7 Food & Water Requirements (refill stops etc) ☐

8 Make Equipment Packing List ☐

9 Camera Equipt, Battery solutions, Safety ☐

10 Location 'Extras': Research-
       (Points of interest,Features, Wildlife etc) ☐

THE PLAN

Date

	MUNRO NAME	My Ref

Meet up time/ location

Area name/ Closest Town

Est. Duration

GPS / Latitude & Longitude / Grid Ref

Est. Distance

Km
Miles

Loop / Line & Back / One Way   Day Trip / Overnight/ Holiday

Local Contact

Accommodation Info

THE EQUIPMENT

A   B

Map Name/No

THE HIKE

Start Time

End Time

Actual Distance

Total No of Steps

Calories
Burned

M   P

POINTS OF INTEREST

Difficulty Level (1 Easy 5 Hard)

Enjoyment Level (1 Bad 5 Good)

Overall Grade (1 Bad 5 Good)

Notes
Facilities
Parking
Costs
Nature
Etc

MY MUNRO TOTAL

THE PLAN

Date

MUNRO NAME

My Ref

Meet up time/ location

Area name/ Closest Town

Est. Duration

GPS / Latitude & Longitude / Grid Ref

Est. Distance

Km
Miles

Loop / Line & Back / One Way   Day Trip / Overnight/ Holiday

Local Contact

Accommodation Info

THE EQUIPMENT

A   B

Map Name/No

THE HIKE

(M) (P)

Start Time

End Time

Actual Distance

Total No of Steps

Calories
Burned

POINTS OF INTEREST

Difficulty Level (1 Easy 5 Hard)

Enjoyment Level (1 Bad 5 Good)

Overall Grade (1 Bad 5 Good)

Notes
Facilities
Parking
Costs
Nature
Etc

MY MUNRO TOTAL

THE PLAN

Date

MUNRO NAME

My Ref

Meet up time/ location	Area name/ Closest Town
Est. Duration	GPS / Latitude & Longitude / Grid Ref
Est. Distance Km Miles	Loop / Line & Back / One Way Day Trip / Overnight/ Holiday
Local Contact	Accommodation Info

THE EQUIPMENT

A   B

Map Name/No

THE HIKE

Start Time

End Time

Actual Distance

Total No of Steps

M   P

POINTS OF INTEREST

Calories
Burned

Difficulty Level (1 Easy 5 Hard) △

Enjoyment Level (1 Bad 5 Good) ♡

Overall Grade (1 Bad 5 Good) ☆

Notes
Facilities
Parking
Costs
Nature
Etc

MY MUNRO TOTAL

THE PLAN

Date

Meet up time/ location	Area name/ Closest Town
Est. Duration	GPS / Latitude & Longitude / Grid Ref
Est. Distance Km Miles	Loop / Line & Back / One Way Day Trip / Overnight/ Holiday
Local Contact	Accommodation Info

MUNRO NAME

My Ref

THE EQUIPMENT

A   B

Map Name/No

THE HIKE

M P	Start Time
	End Time
	Actual Distance
	Total No of Steps Calories Burned

POINTS OF INTEREST

Difficulty Level (1 Easy 5 Hard) △

Enjoyment Level (1 Bad 5 Good) ♡

Overall Grade (1 Bad 5 Good) ☆

Notes
Facilities
Parking
Costs
Nature
Etc

MY MUNRO TOTAL

THE PLAN

	MUNRO NAME	My Ref

Date

Meet up time/ location	Area name/ Closest Town

Est. Duration	GPS / Latitude & Longitude / Grid Ref

Est. Distance	
Km	
Miles	Loop / Line & Back / One Way Day Trip / Overnight/ Holiday

Local Contact	Accommodation Info

THE EQUIPMENT

A   B

Map Name/No

THE HIKE

(M) (P)

Start Time	
End Time	
Actual Distance	
Total No of Steps	

POINTS OF INTEREST

Calories Burned

Difficulty Level (1 Easy 5 Hard)

Enjoyment Level (1 Bad 5 Good)

Overall Grade (1 Bad 5 Good)

Notes
Facilities
Parking
Costs
Nature
Etc

MY MUNRO TOTAL

THE PLAN

Date

Meet up time/ location

Est. Duration

Est. Distance   Km
                                 Miles

Local Contact

MUNRO NAME   My Ref

Area name/ Closest Town

GPS / Latitude & Longitude / Grid Ref

Loop / Line & Back / One Way   Day Trip / Overnight/ Holiday

Accommodation Info

THE EQUIPMENT

A   B

Map Name/No

THE HIKE

(M) (P)

POINTS OF INTEREST

Start Time

End Time

Actual Distance

Total No of Steps

Difficulty Level (1 Easy 5 Hard) △

Enjoyment Level (1 Bad 5 Good) ♡

Overall Grade (1 Bad 5 Good) ☆

Calories
Burned

Notes
Facilities
Parking
Costs
Nature
Etc

MY MUNRO TOTAL

THE PLAN

Date

	MUNRO NAME	My Ref

Meet up time/ location

Area name/ Closest Town

Est. Duration

GPS / Latitude & Longitude / Grid Ref

Est. Distance   Km
                       Miles

Loop / Line & Back / One Way   Day Trip / Overnight/ Holiday

Local Contact

Accommodation Info

THE EQUIPMENT

A   B

Map Name/No

THE HIKE

M   P

Start Time

End Time

Actual Distance

Total No of Steps

Calories
Burned

POINTS OF INTEREST

Difficulty Level (1 Easy 5 Hard) △

Enjoyment Level (1 Bad 5 Good) ♡

Overall Grade (1 Bad 5 Good) ☆

Notes
Facilities
Parking
Costs
Nature
Etc

MY MUNRO TOTAL

THE PLAN

Date

MUNRO NAME

My Ref

Meet up time/ location

Area name/ Closest Town

Est. Duration

GPS / Latitude & Longitude / Grid Ref

Est. Distance

Km
Miles

Loop / Line & Back / One Way   Day Trip / Overnight/ Holiday

Local Contact

Accommodation Info

THE EQUIPMENT

A   B

Map Name/No

THE HIKE

(M) (P)

Start Time

End Time

Actual Distance

Total No of Steps

Calories
Burned

POINTS OF INTEREST

Difficulty Level (1 Easy 5 Hard) △

Enjoyment Level (1 Bad 5 Good) ♡

Overall Grade (1 Bad 5 Good) ☆

Notes
Facilities
Parking
Costs
Nature
Etc

MY MUNRO TOTAL

THE PLAN

Date

MUNRO NAME

My Ref

Meet up time/ location

Area name/ Closest Town

Est. Duration

GPS / Latitude & Longitude / Grid Ref

Est. Distance

Km
Miles

Loop / Line & Back / One Way   Day Trip / Overnight/ Holiday

Local Contact

Accommodation Info

THE EQUIPMENT

A   B

Map Name/No

THE HIKE

Start Time

End Time

M   P

Actual Distance

Total No of Steps

Calories
Burned

POINTS OF INTEREST

Difficulty Level (1 Easy 5 Hard) △

Enjoyment Level (1 Bad 5 Good) ♡

Overall Grade (1 Bad 5 Good) ☆

Notes
Facilities
Parking
Costs
Nature
Etc

MY MUNRO TOTAL

THE PLAN

Date

MUNRO NAME

My Ref

Meet up time/ location

Area name/ Closest Town

Est. Duration

GPS / Latitude & Longitude / Grid Ref

Est. Distance
Km
Miles

Loop / Line & Back / One Way   Day Trip / Overnight/ Holiday

Local Contact

Accommodation Info

THE EQUIPMENT

A   B

Map Name/No

THE HIKE

Start Time

End Time

M   P

Actual Distance

Total No of Steps

Calories
Burned

POINTS OF INTEREST

Difficulty Level (1 Easy 5 Hard)

Enjoyment Level (1 Bad 5 Good)

Overall Grade (1 Bad 5 Good)

Notes
Facilities
Parking
Costs
Nature
Etc

MY MUNRO TOTAL

THE PLAN

Date

MUNRO NAME

My Ref

Meet up time/ location

Area name/ Closest Town

Est. Duration

GPS / Latitude & Longitude / Grid Ref

Est. Distance

Km
Miles

Loop / Line & Back / One Way   Day Trip / Overnight/ Holiday

Local Contact

Accommodation Info

THE EQUIPMENT

A   B

Map Name/No

THE HIKE

(M) (P)

Start Time

End Time

Actual Distance

Total No of Steps

POINTS OF INTEREST

Calories
Burned

Difficulty Level (1 Easy 5 Hard) △

Enjoyment Level (1 Bad 5 Good) ♡

Overall Grade (1 Bad 5 Good) ☆

Notes
Facilities
Parking
Costs
Nature
Etc

MY MUNRO TOTAL

THE PLAN

Date

MUNRO NAME

My Ref

Meet up time/ location

Area name/ Closest Town

Est. Duration

GPS / Latitude & Longitude / Grid Ref

Est. Distance

Km
Miles

Loop / Line & Back / One Way   Day Trip / Overnight/ Holiday

Local Contact

Accommodation Info

THE EQUIPMENT

A   B

Map Name/No

THE HIKE

Start Time

End Time

(M)   (P)

Actual Distance

POINTS OF INTEREST

Total No of Steps

Calories
Burned

Difficulty Level (1 Easy 5 Hard)

Enjoyment Level (1 Bad 5 Good)

Overall Grade (1 Bad 5 Good)

Notes
Facilities
Parking
Costs
Nature
Etc

MY MUNRO TOTAL

THE PLAN

Date

MUNRO NAME	My Ref

Meet up time/ location

Area name/ Closest Town

Est. Duration

GPS / Latitude & Longitude / Grid Ref

Est. Distance

Km
Miles

Loop / Line & Back / One Way   Day Trip / Overnight/ Holiday

Local Contact

Accommodation Info

THE EQUIPMENT

A   B

Map Name/No

THE HIKE

M   P

Start Time

End Time

Actual Distance

Total No of Steps

Calories
Burned

POINTS OF INTEREST

Difficulty Level (1 Easy 5 Hard) △

Enjoyment Level (1 Bad 5 Good) ♡

Overall Grade (1 Bad 5 Good) ☆

Notes
Facilities
Parking
Costs
Nature
Etc

MY MUNRO TOTAL

THE PLAN

MUNRO NAME

My Ref

Date

Meet up time/ location

Area name/ Closest Town

Est. Duration

GPS / Latitude & Longitude / Grid Ref

Est. Distance

Km
Miles

Loop / Line & Back / One Way   Day Trip / Overnight/ Holiday

Local Contact

Accommodation Info

THE EQUIPMENT

A   B

Map Name/No

THE HIKE

M   P

Start Time

End Time

Actual Distance

Total No of Steps

Calories
Burned

POINTS OF INTEREST

Difficulty Level (1 Easy 5 Hard)

Enjoyment Level (1 Bad 5 Good)

Overall Grade (1 Bad 5 Good)

Notes
Facilities
Parking
Costs
Nature
Etc

MY MUNRO TOTAL

THE PLAN

Date

MUNRO NAME

My Ref

Meet up time/ location

Area name/ Closest Town

Est. Duration

GPS / Latitude & Longitude / Grid Ref

Est. Distance

Km
Miles

Loop / Line & Back / One Way   Day Trip / Overnight/ Holiday

Local Contact

Accommodation Info

THE EQUIPMENT

A   B

Map Name/No

THE HIKE

Start Time

End Time

Actual Distance

M   P

Total No of Steps

Calories
Burned

POINTS OF INTEREST

Difficulty Level (1 Easy 5 Hard) △

Enjoyment Level (1 Bad 5 Good) ♡

Overall Grade (1 Bad 5 Good) ☆

Notes
Facilities
Parking
Costs
Nature
Etc

THE PLAN

Date

	MUNRO NAME	My Ref

Meet up time/ location

Est. Duration

Est. Distance _____ Km / Miles

Local Contact

Area name/ Closest Town

GPS / Latitude & Longitude / Grid Ref

Loop / Line & Back / One Way   Day Trip / Overnight/ Holiday

Accommodation Info

THE EQUIPMENT

A   B

Map Name/No

THE HIKE

(M) (P)

Start Time

End Time

Actual Distance

Total No of Steps

Calories Burned

POINTS OF INTEREST

Difficulty Level (1 Easy 5 Hard) △

Enjoyment Level (1 Bad 5 Good) ♡

Overall Grade (1 Bad 5 Good) ☆

Notes
Facilities
Parking
Costs
Nature
Etc

MY MUNRO TOTAL

THE PLAN

	MUNRO NAME	My Ref
Date		

Meet up time/ location	Area name/ Closest Town
Est. Duration	GPS / Latitude & Longitude / Grid Ref
Est. Distance — Km Miles	
	Loop / Line & Back / One Way Day Trip / Overnight/ Holiday
Local Contact	Accommodation Info

THE EQUIPMENT

A   B

Map Name/No

THE HIKE

Start Time

End Time

M   P

Actual Distance

Total No of Steps

Calories Burned

POINTS OF INTEREST

Difficulty Level (1 Easy 5 Hard) △

Enjoyment Level (1 Bad 5 Good) ♡

Overall Grade (1 Bad 5 Good) ☆

Notes
Facilities
Parking
Costs
Nature
Etc

MY MUNRO TOTAL

THE PLAN

Date

MUNRO NAME

My Ref

Meet up time/ location

Area name/ Closest Town

Est. Duration

GPS / Latitude & Longitude / Grid Ref

Est. Distance

Km
Miles

Loop / Line & Back / One Way   Day Trip / Overnight/ Holiday

Local Contact

Accommodation Info

THE EQUIPMENT

A   B

Map Name/No

THE HIKE

M   P

Start Time

End Time

Actual Distance

Total No of Steps

Calories
Burned

POINTS OF INTEREST

Difficulty Level (1 Easy 5 Hard) △

Enjoyment Level (1 Bad 5 Good) ♡

Overall Grade (1 Bad 5 Good) ☆

Notes
Facilities
Parking
Costs
Nature
Etc

MY MUNRO TOTAL

THE PLAN

Date

MUNRO NAME	My Ref

Meet up time/ location

Area name/ Closest Town

Est. Duration

GPS / Latitude & Longitude / Grid Ref

Est. Distance

Km
Miles

Loop / Line & Back / One Way   Day Trip / Overnight/ Holiday

Local Contact

Accommodation Info

THE EQUIPMENT

A   B

Map Name/No

THE HIKE

(M)   (P)

Start Time

End Time

Actual Distance

Total No of Steps

Calories
Burned

POINTS OF INTEREST

Difficulty Level (1 Easy 5 Hard) △

Enjoyment Level (1 Bad 5 Good) ♡

Overall Grade (1 Bad 5 Good) ☆

Notes
Facilities
Parking
Costs
Nature
Etc

MY MUNRO TOTAL

THE PLAN

Date	MUNRO NAME
	My Ref

Meet up time/ location	Area name/ Closest Town
Est. Duration	GPS / Latitude & Longitude / Grid Ref
Est. Distance Km / Miles	Loop / Line & Back / One Way Day Trip / Overnight/ Holiday
Local Contact	Accommodation Info

THE EQUIPMENT

A   B

Map Name/No

THE HIKE

Start Time

End Time

(M) (P)

Actual Distance

POINTS OF INTEREST

Total No of Steps

Calories Burned

Difficulty Level (1 Easy 5 Hard) △

Enjoyment Level (1 Bad 5 Good) ♡

Overall Grade (1 Bad 5 Good) ☆

Notes
Facilities
Parking
Costs
Nature
Etc

MY MUNRO TOTAL

THE PLAN

MUNRO NAME

My Ref

Date

Meet up time/ location

Area name/ Closest Town

Est. Duration

GPS / Latitude & Longitude / Grid Ref

Est. Distance

Km
Miles

Loop / Line & Back / One Way   Day Trip / Overnight/ Holiday

Local Contact

Accommodation Info

THE EQUIPMENT

A   B

Map Name/No

THE HIKE

Start Time

End Time

M   P

Actual Distance

Total No of Steps

Calories
Burned

POINTS OF INTEREST

Difficulty Level (1 Easy 5 Hard)

Enjoyment Level (1 Bad 5 Good)

Overall Grade (1 Bad 5 Good)

Notes
Facilities
Parking
Costs
Nature
Etc

MY MUNRO TOTAL

THE PLAN

Date

	MUNRO NAME	My Ref

Meet up time/ location

Area name/ Closest Town

Est. Duration

GPS / Latitude & Longitude / Grid Ref

Est. Distance

Km
Miles

Loop / Line & Back / One Way   Day Trip / Overnight/ Holiday

Local Contact

Accommodation Info

THE EQUIPMENT

A   B

Map Name/No

THE HIKE

(M) (P)

Start Time

End Time

Actual Distance

Total No of Steps

Calories
Burned

POINTS OF INTEREST

Difficulty Level (1 Easy 5 Hard) △

Enjoyment Level (1 Bad 5 Good) ♡

Overall Grade (1 Bad 5 Good) ☆

Notes
Facilities
Parking
Costs
Nature
Etc

MY MUNRO TOTAL

THE PLAN

Date

MUNRO NAME

My Ref

Meet up time/ location

Area name/ Closest Town

Est. Duration

GPS / Latitude & Longitude / Grid Ref

Est. Distance

Km
Miles

Loop / Line & Back / One Way   Day Trip / Overnight/ Holiday

Local Contact

Accommodation Info

THE EQUIPMENT

A   B

Map Name/No

THE HIKE

Start Time

End Time

Actual Distance

Total No of Steps

Calories
Burned

POINTS OF INTEREST

Difficulty Level (1 Easy 5 Hard)

Enjoyment Level (1 Bad 5 Good)

Overall Grade (1 Bad 5 Good)

Notes
Facilities
Parking
Costs
Nature
Etc

MY MUNRO TOTAL

THE PLAN

Date

MUNRO NAME

My Ref

Meet up time/ location

Area name/ Closest Town

Est. Duration

GPS / Latitude & Longitude / Grid Ref

Est. Distance

Km
Miles

Loop / Line & Back / One Way   Day Trip / Overnight/ Holiday

Local Contact

Accommodation Info

THE EQUIPMENT

A   B

Map Name/No

THE HIKE

Start Time

End Time

Actual Distance

M   P

Total No of Steps

POINTS OF INTEREST

Calories
Burned

Difficulty Level (1 Easy 5 Hard) △

Enjoyment Level (1 Bad 5 Good) ♡

Overall Grade (1 Bad 5 Good) ☆

Notes
Facilities
Parking
Costs
Nature
Etc

MY MUNRO TOTAL

THE PLAN

Date

MUNRO NAME		My Ref

Meet up time/ location

Area name/ Closest Town

Est. Duration

GPS / Latitude & Longitude / Grid Ref

Est. Distance   Km
                     Miles

Loop / Line & Back / One Way   Day Trip / Overnight/ Holiday

Local Contact

Accommodation Info

THE EQUIPMENT

A   B

Map Name/No

THE HIKE

M   P

Start Time

End Time

Actual Distance

Total No of Steps

Calories
Burned

POINTS OF INTEREST

Difficulty Level (1 Easy 5 Hard)   △

Enjoyment Level (1 Bad 5 Good)   ♡

Overall Grade (1 Bad 5 Good)   ☆

Notes
Facilities
Parking
Costs
Nature
Etc

MY MUNRO TOTAL

THE PLAN

Date

MUNRO NAME

My Ref

Meet up time/ location

Area name/ Closest Town

Est. Duration

GPS / Latitude & Longitude / Grid Ref

Est. Distance

Km
Miles

Loop / Line & Back / One Way   Day Trip / Overnight/ Holiday

Local Contact

Accommodation Info

THE EQUIPMENT

A   B

Map Name/No

THE HIKE

M   P

Start Time

End Time

Actual Distance

Total No of Steps

Calories
Burned

POINTS OF INTEREST

Difficulty Level (1 Easy 5 Hard) △

Enjoyment Level (1 Bad 5 Good) ♡

Overall Grade (1 Bad 5 Good) ☆

Notes
Facilities
Parking
Costs
Nature
Etc

MY MUNRO TOTAL

THE PLAN

Date

MUNRO NAME

My Ref

Meet up time/ location

Area name/ Closest Town

Est. Duration

GPS / Latitude & Longitude / Grid Ref

Est. Distance

Km
Miles

Loop / Line & Back / One Way   Day Trip / Overnight/ Holiday

Local Contact

Accommodation Info

THE EQUIPMENT

A   B

Map Name/No

THE HIKE

Start Time

End Time

(M)   (P)

Actual Distance

POINTS OF INTEREST

Total No of Steps

Calories
Burned

Difficulty Level (1 Easy 5 Hard) △

Enjoyment Level (1 Bad 5 Good) ♡

Overall Grade (1 Bad 5 Good) ☆

Notes
Facilities
Parking
Costs
Nature
Etc

MY MUNRO TOTAL

THE PLAN

Date

MUNRO NAME	My Ref

Meet up time/ location

Area name/ Closest Town

Est. Duration

GPS / Latitude & Longitude / Grid Ref

Est. Distance   Km Miles

Loop / Line & Back / One Way   Day Trip / Overnight/ Holiday

Local Contact

Accommodation Info

THE EQUIPMENT

A   B

Map Name/No

THE HIKE

(M) (P)

Start Time

End Time

Actual Distance

Total No of Steps

Calories Burned

POINTS OF INTEREST

Difficulty Level (1 Easy 5 Hard) △

Enjoyment Level (1 Bad 5 Good) ♡

Overall Grade (1 Bad 5 Good) ☆

Notes
Facilities
Parking
Costs
Nature
Etc

MY MUNRO TOTAL

THE PLAN

MUNRO NAME

My Ref

Date

Meet up time/ location

Area name/ Closest Town

Est. Duration

GPS / Latitude & Longitude / Grid Ref

Est. Distance

Km
Miles

Loop / Line & Back / One Way   Day Trip / Overnight/ Holiday

Local Contact

Accommodation Info

THE EQUIPMENT

A B

Map Name/No

THE HIKE

Start Time

End Time

Actual Distance

(M) (P)

POINTS OF INTEREST

Total No of Steps

Calories
Burned

Difficulty Level (1 Easy 5 Hard) △

Enjoyment Level (1 Bad 5 Good) ♡

Overall Grade (1 Bad 5 Good) ☆

Notes
Facilities
Parking
Costs
Nature
Etc

MY MUNRO TOTAL

THE PLAN

	MUNRO NAME	My Ref
Date		

Meet up time/ location	Area name/ Closest Town
Est. Duration	GPS / Latitude & Longitude / Grid Ref
Est. Distance Km Miles	Loop / Line & Back / One Way Day Trip / Overnight/ Holiday
Local Contact	Accommodation Info

THE EQUIPMENT

A B

Map Name/No

THE HIKE

Start Time

End Time

Actual Distance

Total No of Steps

Calories
Burned

(M) (P)

POINTS OF INTEREST

Difficulty Level (1 Easy 5 Hard) △

Enjoyment Level (1 Bad 5 Good) ♡

Overall Grade (1 Bad 5 Good) ☆

Notes
Facilities
Parking
Costs
Nature
Etc

MY MUNRO TOTAL

THE PLAN

MUNRO NAME

My Ref

Date

Meet up time/ location	Area name/ Closest Town

Est. Duration	GPS / Latitude & Longitude / Grid Ref

Est. Distance	Km	Miles

Loop / Line & Back / One Way   Day Trip / Overnight/ Holiday

Local Contact	Accommodation Info

THE EQUIPMENT

A   B

Map Name/No

THE HIKE

Start Time

End Time

Actual Distance

Total No of Steps

Calories Burned

POINTS OF INTEREST

Difficulty Level (1 Easy 5 Hard) △

Enjoyment Level (1 Bad 5 Good) ♡

Overall Grade (1 Bad 5 Good) ☆

Notes
Facilities
Parking
Costs
Nature
Etc

MY MUNRO TOTAL

THE PLAN

Date

MUNRO NAME	My Ref

Meet up time/ location

Area name/ Closest Town

Est. Duration

GPS / Latitude & Longitude / Grid Ref

Est. Distance   Km
                       Miles

Loop / Line & Back / One Way   Day Trip / Overnight/ Holiday

Local Contact

Accommodation Info

THE EQUIPMENT

A   B

Map Name/No

THE HIKE

(M) (P)

Start Time

End Time

Actual Distance

Total No of Steps

Calories
Burned

POINTS OF INTEREST

Difficulty Level (1 Easy 5 Hard) △

Enjoyment Level (1 Bad 5 Good) ♡

Overall Grade (1 Bad 5 Good) ☆

Notes
Facilities
Parking
Costs
Nature
Etc

MY MUNRO TOTAL

THE PLAN

Date

MUNRO NAME

My Ref

Meet up time/ location

Area name/ Closest Town

Est. Duration

GPS / Latitude & Longitude / Grid Ref

Est. Distance

Km
Miles

Loop / Line & Back / One Way   Day Trip / Overnight/ Holiday

Local Contact

Accommodation Info

THE EQUIPMENT

A   B

Map Name/No

THE HIKE

M   P

Start Time

End Time

Actual Distance

Total No of Steps

Calories
Burned

POINTS OF INTEREST

Difficulty Level (1 Easy 5 Hard) △

Enjoyment Level (1 Bad 5 Good) ♡

Overall Grade (1 Bad 5 Good) ☆

Notes
Facilities
Parking
Costs
Nature
Etc

MY MUNRO TOTAL

THE PLAN

Date

| MUNRO NAME | My Ref |

Meet up time/ location

Area name/ Closest Town

Est. Duration

GPS / Latitude & Longitude / Grid Ref

Est. Distance
Km
Miles

Loop / Line & Back / One Way   Day Trip / Overnight/ Holiday

Local Contact

Accommodation Info

THE EQUIPMENT

A   B

Map Name/No

THE HIKE

M   P

Start Time

End Time

Actual Distance

Total No of Steps

Calories Burned

POINTS OF INTEREST

Difficulty Level (1 Easy 5 Hard) △

Enjoyment Level (1 Bad 5 Good) ♡

Overall Grade (1 Bad 5 Good) ☆

Notes
Facilities
Parking
Costs
Nature
Etc

MY MUNRO TOTAL

THE PLAN

Date

	MUNRO NAME	My Ref

Meet up time/ location

Area name/ Closest Town

Est. Duration

GPS / Latitude & Longitude / Grid Ref

Est. Distance

Km
Miles

Loop / Line & Back / One Way   Day Trip / Overnight/ Holiday

Local Contact

Accommodation Info

THE EQUIPMENT

A   B

Map Name/No

THE HIKE

Start Time

End Time

Actual Distance

Total No of Steps

Calories Burned

(M) (P)

POINTS OF INTEREST

Difficulty Level (1 Easy 5 Hard) △

Enjoyment Level (1 Bad 5 Good) ♡

Overall Grade (1 Bad 5 Good) ☆

Notes
Facilities
Parking
Costs
Nature
Etc

MY MUNRO TOTAL

THE PLAN

Date

MUNRO NAME

My Ref

Meet up time/ location

Area name/ Closest Town

Est. Duration

GPS / Latitude & Longitude / Grid Ref

Est. Distance

Km
Miles

Loop / Line & Back / One Way   Day Trip / Overnight/ Holiday

Local Contact

Accommodation Info

THE EQUIPMENT

A   B

Map Name/No

THE HIKE

M   P

Start Time

End Time

Actual Distance

Total No of Steps

Calories
Burned

POINTS OF INTEREST

Difficulty Level (1 Easy 5 Hard)

Enjoyment Level (1 Bad 5 Good)

Overall Grade (1 Bad 5 Good)

Notes
Facilities
Parking
Costs
Nature
Etc

MY MUNRO TOTAL

THE PLAN

Date

	MUNRO NAME	My Ref

Meet up time/ location

Area name/ Closest Town

Est. Duration

GPS / Latitude & Longitude / Grid Ref

Est. Distance

Km
Miles

Loop / Line & Back / One Way   Day Trip / Overnight/ Holiday

Local Contact

Accommodation Info

THE EQUIPMENT

A   B

Map Name/No

THE HIKE

(M) (P)

Start Time

End Time

Actual Distance

Total No of Steps

POINTS OF INTEREST

Calories
Burned

Difficulty Level (1 Easy 5 Hard) △

Enjoyment Level (1 Bad 5 Good) ♡

Overall Grade (1 Bad 5 Good) ☆

Notes
Facilities
Parking
Costs
Nature
Etc

MY MUNRO TOTAL

THE PLAN

MUNRO NAME

My Ref

Date

Meet up time/ location

Area name/ Closest Town

Est. Duration

GPS / Latitude & Longitude / Grid Ref

Est. Distance

Km
Miles

Loop / Line & Back / One Way   Day Trip / Overnight/ Holiday

Local Contact

Accommodation Info

THE EQUIPMENT

A   B

Map Name/No

THE HIKE

Start Time

End Time

M   P

Actual Distance

POINTS OF INTEREST

Total No of Steps

Calories
Burned

Difficulty Level (1 Easy 5 Hard)

Enjoyment Level (1 Bad 5 Good)

Overall Grade (1 Bad 5 Good)

Notes
Facilities
Parking
Costs
Nature
Etc

MY MUNRO TOTAL

THE PLAN

Date

MUNRO NAME

My Ref

Meet up time/ location

Area name/ Closest Town

Est. Duration

GPS / Latitude & Longitude / Grid Ref

Est. Distance

Km
Miles

Loop / Line & Back / One Way   Day Trip / Overnight/ Holiday

Local Contact

Accommodation Info

THE EQUIPMENT

A   B

Map Name/No

THE HIKE

M   P

Start Time

End Time

Actual Distance

Total No of Steps

POINTS OF INTEREST

Calories
Burned

Difficulty Level (1 Easy 5 Hard) △

Enjoyment Level (1 Bad 5 Good) ♡

Overall Grade (1 Bad 5 Good) ☆

Notes
Facilities
Parking
Costs
Nature
Etc

MY MUNRO TOTAL

THE PLAN

Date

	MUNRO NAME	My Ref

Meet up time/ location

Area name/ Closest Town

Est. Duration

GPS / Latitude & Longitude / Grid Ref

Est. Distance   Km
                            Miles

Loop / Line & Back / One Way   Day Trip / Overnight/ Holiday

Local Contact

Accommodation Info

THE EQUIPMENT

A   B

Map Name/No

THE HIKE

(M) (P)

Start Time

End Time

Actual Distance

Total No of Steps   Calories
                                      Burned

POINTS OF INTEREST

Difficulty Level (1 Easy 5 Hard) △

Enjoyment Level (1 Bad 5 Good) ♡

Overall Grade (1 Bad 5 Good) ☆

Notes
Facilities
Parking
Costs
Nature
Etc

MY MUNRO TOTAL

THE PLAN

THE PLAN	**MUNRO NAME**
Date	

My Ref

Meet up time/ location

Area name/ Closest Town

Est. Duration

GPS / Latitude & Longitude / Grid Ref

Est. Distance

Km
Miles

Loop / Line & Back / One Way   Day Trip / Overnight/ Holiday

Local Contact

Accommodation Info

THE EQUIPMENT

A   B

Map Name/No

THE HIKE

Start Time

End Time

Actual Distance

(M) (P)

Total No of Steps

Calories
Burned

POINTS OF INTEREST

Difficulty Level (1 Easy 5 Hard) △

Enjoyment Level (1 Bad 5 Good) ♡

Overall Grade (1 Bad 5 Good) ☆

Notes
Facilities
Parking
Costs
Nature
Etc

MY MUNRO TOTAL

THE PLAN

Date

MUNRO NAME

My Ref

Meet up time/ location

Area name/ Closest Town

Est. Duration

GPS / Latitude & Longitude / Grid Ref

Est. Distance

Km
Miles

Loop / Line & Back / One Way   Day Trip / Overnight/ Holiday

Local Contact

Accommodation Info

THE EQUIPMENT

A   B

Map Name/No

THE HIKE

Start Time

End Time

Actual Distance

Total No of Steps

Calories
Burned

(M)   (P)

POINTS OF INTEREST

Difficulty Level (1 Easy 5 Hard)

Enjoyment Level (1 Bad 5 Good)

Overall Grade (1 Bad 5 Good)

Notes
Facilities
Parking
Costs
Nature
Etc

MY MUNRO TOTAL

THE PLAN

Date

MUNRO NAME	My Ref

Meet up time/ location

Area name/ Closest Town

Est. Duration

GPS / Latitude & Longitude / Grid Ref

Est. Distance

Km
Miles

Loop / Line & Back / One Way   Day Trip / Overnight/ Holiday

Local Contact

Accommodation Info

THE EQUIPMENT

A   B

Map Name/No

THE HIKE

Start Time

End Time

Actual Distance

Total No of Steps

M   P

POINTS OF INTEREST

Calories
Burned

Difficulty Level (1 Easy 5 Hard) △

Enjoyment Level (1 Bad 5 Good) ♡

Overall Grade (1 Bad 5 Good) ☆

Notes
Facilities
Parking
Costs
Nature
Etc

MY MUNRO TOTAL

THE PLAN

Date

MUNRO NAME

My Ref

Meet up time/ location

Area name/ Closest Town

Est. Duration

GPS / Latitude & Longitude / Grid Ref

Est. Distance

Km
Miles

Loop / Line & Back / One Way   Day Trip / Overnight/ Holiday

Local Contact

Accommodation Info

THE EQUIPMENT

A   B

Map Name/No

THE HIKE

M   P

Start Time

End Time

Actual Distance

Total No of Steps

Calories
Burned

POINTS OF INTEREST

Difficulty Level (1 Easy 5 Hard) △

Enjoyment Level (1 Bad 5 Good) ♡

Overall Grade (1 Bad 5 Good) ☆

Notes
Facilities
Parking
Costs
Nature
Etc

MY MUNRO TOTAL

THE PLAN

Date

MUNRO NAME

My Ref

| Meet up time/ location | Area name/ Closest Town |

| Est. Duration | GPS / Latitude & Longitude / Grid Ref |

| Est. Distance | Km Miles |

Loop / Line & Back / One Way   Day Trip / Overnight/ Holiday

| Local Contact | Accommodation Info |

THE EQUIPMENT

A   B

Map Name/No

THE HIKE

(M) (P)

Start Time

End Time

Actual Distance

Total No of Steps

POINTS OF INTEREST

Calories Burned

Difficulty Level (1 Easy 5 Hard) △

Enjoyment Level (1 Bad 5 Good) ♡

Overall Grade (1 Bad 5 Good) ☆

Notes
Facilities
Parking
Costs
Nature
Etc

MY MUNRO TOTAL

THE PLAN

Date

Meet up time/ location

Est. Duration

Est. Distance

Km
Miles

Local Contact

MUNRO NAME

My Ref

Area name/ Closest Town

GPS / Latitude & Longitude / Grid Ref

Loop / Line & Back / One Way   Day Trip / Overnight/ Holiday

Accommodation Info

THE EQUIPMENT

A B

Map Name/No

THE HIKE

(M) (P)

Start Time

End Time

Actual Distance

Total No of Steps

Calories
Burned

POINTS OF INTEREST

Difficulty Level (1 Easy 5 Hard) △

Enjoyment Level (1 Bad 5 Good) ♡

Overall Grade (1 Bad 5 Good) ☆

Notes
Facilities
Parking
Costs
Nature
Etc

MY MUNRO TOTAL

THE PLAN

Date

MUNRO NAME

My Ref

Meet up time/ location

Area name/ Closest Town

Est. Duration

GPS / Latitude & Longitude / Grid Ref

Est. Distance

Km
Miles

Loop / Line & Back / One Way   Day Trip / Overnight/ Holiday

Local Contact

Accommodation Info

THE EQUIPMENT

A   B

Map Name/No

THE HIKE

Start Time

End Time

M   P

Actual Distance

Total No of Steps

POINTS OF INTEREST

Calories
Burned

Difficulty Level (1 Easy 5 Hard)

Enjoyment Level (1 Bad 5 Good)

Overall Grade (1 Bad 5 Good)

Notes
Facilities
Parking
Costs
Nature
Etc

MY MUNRO TOTAL

THE PLAN

MUNRO NAME		My Ref

Date

Meet up time/ location

Area name/ Closest Town

Est. Duration

GPS / Latitude & Longitude / Grid Ref

Est. Distance

Km
Miles

Loop / Line & Back / One Way   Day Trip / Overnight/ Holiday

Local Contact

Accommodation Info

THE EQUIPMENT

A   B

Map Name/No

THE HIKE

M   P

Start Time

End Time

Actual Distance

Total No of Steps

Calories
Burned

POINTS OF INTEREST

Difficulty Level (1 Easy 5 Hard) △

Enjoyment Level (1 Bad 5 Good) ♡

Overall Grade (1 Bad 5 Good) ☆

Notes
Facilities
Parking
Costs
Nature
Etc

MY MUNRO TOTAL

THE PLAN

Date

MUNRO NAME

My Ref

Meet up time/ location

Area name/ Closest Town

Est. Duration

GPS / Latitude & Longitude / Grid Ref

Est. Distance

Km
Miles

Loop / Line & Back / One Way   Day Trip / Overnight/ Holiday

Local Contact

Accommodation Info

THE EQUIPMENT

A   B

Map Name/No

THE HIKE

Start Time

End Time

M   P

Actual Distance

Total No of Steps

Calories
Burned

POINTS OF INTEREST

Difficulty Level (1 Easy 5 Hard) △

Enjoyment Level (1 Bad 5 Good) ♡

Overall Grade (1 Bad 5 Good) ☆

Notes
Facilities
Parking
Costs
Nature
Etc

MY MUNRO TOTAL

THE PLAN

Date

MUNRO NAME

My Ref

Meet up time/ location

Area name/ Closest Town

Est. Duration

GPS / Latitude & Longitude / Grid Ref

Est. Distance

Km
Miles

Loop / Line & Back / One Way   Day Trip / Overnight/ Holiday

Local Contact

Accommodation Info

THE EQUIPMENT

A B

Map Name/No

THE HIKE

Start Time

End Time

(M) (P)

Actual Distance

Total No of Steps

Calories
Burned

POINTS OF INTEREST

Difficulty Level (1 Easy 5 Hard) △

Enjoyment Level (1 Bad 5 Good) ♡

Overall Grade (1 Bad 5 Good) ☆

Notes
Facilities
Parking
Costs
Nature
Etc

MY MUNRO TOTAL

THE PLAN

Date

MUNRO NAME	My Ref

Meet up time/ location

Area name/ Closest Town

Est. Duration

GPS / Latitude & Longitude / Grid Ref

Est. Distance

Km
Miles

Loop / Line & Back / One Way   Day Trip / Overnight/ Holiday

Local Contact

Accommodation Info

THE EQUIPMENT

A   B

Map Name/No

THE HIKE

Start Time

End Time

M   P

Actual Distance

Total No of Steps

POINTS OF INTEREST

Calories
Burned

Difficulty Level (1 Easy 5 Hard) △

Enjoyment Level (1 Bad 5 Good) ♡

Overall Grade (1 Bad 5 Good) ☆

Notes
Facilities
Parking
Costs
Nature
Etc

MY MUNRO TOTAL

THE PLAN

Date

MUNRO NAME		My Ref

Meet up time/ location

Area name/ Closest Town

Est. Duration

GPS / Latitude & Longitude / Grid Ref

Est. Distance

Km
Miles

Loop / Line & Back / One Way   Day Trip / Overnight/ Holiday

Local Contact

Accommodation Info

THE EQUIPMENT

A   B

Map Name/No

THE HIKE

(M)   (P)

Start Time

End Time

Actual Distance

Total No of Steps

Calories
Burned

POINTS OF INTEREST

Difficulty Level (1 Easy 5 Hard) △

Enjoyment Level (1 Bad 5 Good) ♡

Overall Grade (1 Bad 5 Good) ☆

Notes
Facilities
Parking
Costs
Nature
Etc

MY MUNRO TOTAL

THE PLAN

MUNRO NAME	**My Ref**

Date

Meet up time/ location

Area name/ Closest Town

Est. Duration

GPS / Latitude & Longitude / Grid Ref

Est. Distance

Km
Miles

Loop / Line & Back / One Way   Day Trip / Overnight/ Holiday

Local Contact

Accommodation Info

THE EQUIPMENT

A   B

Map Name/No

THE HIKE

(M) (P)

Start Time

End Time

Actual Distance

Total No of Steps

Calories
Burned

POINTS OF INTEREST

Difficulty Level (1 Easy 5 Hard) △

Enjoyment Level (1 Bad 5 Good) ♡

Overall Grade (1 Bad 5 Good) ☆

Notes
Facilities
Parking
Costs
Nature
Etc

MY MUNRO TOTAL

THE PLAN

Date

MUNRO NAME

My Ref

Meet up time/ location

Area name/ Closest Town

Est. Duration

GPS / Latitude & Longitude / Grid Ref

Est. Distance

Km
Miles

Loop / Line & Back / One Way   Day Trip / Overnight/ Holiday

Local Contact

Accommodation Info

THE EQUIPMENT

A   B

Map Name/No

THE HIKE

Start Time

End Time

Actual Distance

Total No of Steps

Calories
Burned

POINTS OF INTEREST

Difficulty Level (1 Easy 5 Hard)

Enjoyment Level (1 Bad 5 Good)

Overall Grade (1 Bad 5 Good)

Notes
Facilities
Parking
Costs
Nature
Etc

MY MUNRO TOTAL

THE PLAN

MUNRO NAME	My Ref

Date

Meet up time/ location	Area name/ Closest Town

Est. Duration	GPS / Latitude & Longitude / Grid Ref

Est. Distance   Km
                       Miles

Loop / Line & Back / One Way   Day Trip / Overnight/ Holiday

Local Contact	Accommodation Info

THE EQUIPMENT

A   B

Map Name/No

THE HIKE

Start Time

End Time

M   P

Actual Distance

Total No of Steps   Calories
                                 Burned

POINTS OF INTEREST

Difficulty Level (1 Easy 5 Hard) △

Enjoyment Level (1 Bad 5 Good) ♡

Overall Grade (1 Bad 5 Good) ☆

Notes
Facilities
Parking
Costs
Nature
Etc

MY MUNRO TOTAL

THE PLAN

Date

MUNRO NAME	My Ref

Meet up time/ location

Area name/ Closest Town

Est. Duration

GPS / Latitude & Longitude / Grid Ref

Est. Distance   Km
                                 Miles

Loop / Line & Back / One Way   Day Trip / Overnight/ Holiday

Local Contact

Accommodation Info

THE EQUIPMENT

A   B

Map Name/No

THE HIKE

M   P

Start Time

End Time

Actual Distance

Total No of Steps

Calories
Burned

POINTS OF INTEREST

Difficulty Level (1 Easy 5 Hard)

Enjoyment Level (1 Bad 5 Good)

Overall Grade (1 Bad 5 Good)

Notes
Facilities
Parking
Costs
Nature
Etc

MY MUNRO TOTAL

THE PLAN

Date

| | MUNRO NAME | My Ref |

Meet up time/ location

Area name/ Closest Town

Est. Duration

GPS / Latitude & Longitude / Grid Ref

Est. Distance

Km
Miles

Loop / Line & Back / One Way   Day Trip / Overnight/ Holiday

Local Contact

Accommodation Info

THE EQUIPMENT

A B

Map Name/No

THE HIKE

Start Time

End Time

Actual Distance

(M) (P)

Total No of Steps

POINTS OF INTEREST

Calories
Burned

Difficulty Level (1 Easy 5 Hard) △

Enjoyment Level (1 Bad 5 Good) ♡

Overall Grade (1 Bad 5 Good) ☆

Notes
Facilities
Parking
Costs
Nature
Etc

MY MUNRO TOTAL

THE PLAN

Date

Meet up time/ location

Est. Duration

Est. Distance

Km
Miles

Local Contact

MUNRO NAME

My Ref

Area name/ Closest Town

GPS / Latitude & Longitude / Grid Ref

Loop / Line & Back / One Way   Day Trip / Overnight/ Holiday

Accommodation Info

THE EQUIPMENT

A   B

Map Name/No

THE HIKE

Start Time

End Time

Actual Distance

Total No of Steps

Calories
Burned

M   P

POINTS OF INTEREST

Difficulty Level (1 Easy 5 Hard) △

Enjoyment Level (1 Bad 5 Good) ♡

Overall Grade (1 Bad 5 Good) ☆

Notes
Facilities
Parking
Costs
Nature
Etc

MY MUNRO TOTAL

THE PLAN

Date

| MUNRO NAME | My Ref |

Meet up time/ location

Area name/ Closest Town

Est. Duration

GPS / Latitude & Longitude / Grid Ref

Est. Distance

Km
Miles

Loop / Line & Back / One Way   Day Trip / Overnight/ Holiday

Local Contact

Accommodation Info

THE EQUIPMENT

A B

Map Name/No

THE HIKE

Start Time

End Time

Actual Distance

Total No of Steps

(M) (P)

POINTS OF INTEREST

Calories
Burned

Difficulty Level (1 Easy 5 Hard) △

Enjoyment Level (1 Bad 5 Good) ♡

Overall Grade (1 Bad 5 Good) ☆

Notes
Facilities
Parking
Costs
Nature
Etc

MY MUNRO TOTAL

THE PLAN

| MUNRO NAME | My Ref |

Date

Meet up time/ location

Area name/ Closest Town

Est. Duration

GPS / Latitude & Longitude / Grid Ref

Est. Distance

Km
Miles

Loop / Line & Back / One Way   Day Trip / Overnight/ Holiday

Local Contact

Accommodation Info

THE EQUIPMENT

A   B

Map Name/No

THE HIKE

Start Time

End Time

(M) (P)

Actual Distance

Total No of Steps

Calories
Burned

POINTS OF INTEREST

Difficulty Level (1 Easy 5 Hard)

Enjoyment Level (1 Bad 5 Good)

Overall Grade (1 Bad 5 Good)

Notes
Facilities
Parking
Costs
Nature
Etc

MY MUNRO TOTAL

THE PLAN

MUNRO NAME

My Ref

Date

Meet up time/ location

Area name/ Closest Town

Est. Duration

GPS / Latitude & Longitude / Grid Ref

Est. Distance

Km
Miles

Loop / Line & Back / One Way   Day Trip / Overnight/ Holiday

Local Contact

Accommodation Info

THE EQUIPMENT

A   B

Map Name/No

THE HIKE

M   P

Start Time

End Time

Actual Distance

Total No of Steps

Calories
Burned

POINTS OF INTEREST

Difficulty Level (1 Easy 5 Hard)

Enjoyment Level (1 Bad 5 Good)

Overall Grade (1 Bad 5 Good)

Notes
Facilities
Parking
Costs
Nature
Etc

MY MUNRO TOTAL

THE PLAN

Date

MUNRO NAME	My Ref

Meet up time/ location

Area name/ Closest Town

Est. Duration

GPS / Latitude & Longitude / Grid Ref

Est. Distance   Km Miles

Loop / Line & Back / One Way   Day Trip / Overnight/ Holiday

Local Contact

Accommodation Info

THE EQUIPMENT

A B

Map Name/No

THE HIKE

(M) (P)

Start Time

End Time

Actual Distance

Total No of Steps

Calories Burned

POINTS OF INTEREST

Difficulty Level (1 Easy 5 Hard) △

Enjoyment Level (1 Bad 5 Good) ♡

Overall Grade (1 Bad 5 Good) ☆

Notes
Facilities
Parking
Costs
Nature
Etc

MY MUNRO TOTAL

THE PLAN

Date

MUNRO NAME

My Ref

Meet up time/ location

Area name/ Closest Town

Est. Duration

GPS / Latitude & Longitude / Grid Ref

Est. Distance

Km
Miles

Loop / Line & Back / One Way   Day Trip / Overnight/ Holiday

Local Contact

Accommodation Info

THE EQUIPMENT

A   B

Map Name/No

THE HIKE

Start Time

End Time

Actual Distance

M   P

Total No of Steps

Calories
Burned

POINTS OF INTEREST

Difficulty Level (1 Easy 5 Hard) △

Enjoyment Level (1 Bad 5 Good) ♡

Overall Grade (1 Bad 5 Good) ☆

Notes
Facilities
Parking
Costs
Nature
Etc

MY MUNRO TOTAL

THE PLAN

Date

Meet up time/ location

Est. Duration

Est. Distance
Km
Miles

Local Contact

MUNRO NAME

My Ref

Area name/ Closest Town

GPS / Latitude & Longitude / Grid Ref

Loop / Line & Back / One Way   Day Trip / Overnight/ Holiday

Accommodation Info

THE EQUIPMENT

A   B

Map Name/No

THE HIKE

Start Time

End Time

Actual Distance

Total No of Steps

Calories
Burned

POINTS OF INTEREST

Difficulty Level (1 Easy 5 Hard) △

Enjoyment Level (1 Bad 5 Good) ♡

Overall Grade (1 Bad 5 Good) ☆

Notes
Facilities
Parking
Costs
Nature
Etc

MY MUNRO TOTAL

THE PLAN

Date

| MUNRO NAME | My Ref |

Meet up time/ location

Area name/ Closest Town

Est. Duration

GPS / Latitude & Longitude / Grid Ref

Est. Distance

Km
Miles

Loop / Line & Back / One Way   Day Trip / Overnight/ Holiday

Local Contact

Accommodation Info

THE EQUIPMENT

A   B

Map Name/No

THE HIKE

Start Time

End Time

Actual Distance

Total No of Steps

(M)   (P)

Calories
Burned

POINTS OF INTEREST

Difficulty Level (1 Easy 5 Hard) △

Enjoyment Level (1 Bad 5 Good) ♡

Overall Grade (1 Bad 5 Good) ☆

Notes
Facilities
Parking
Costs
Nature
Etc

MY MUNRO TOTAL

THE PLAN

MUNRO NAME	**My Ref**

Date

Meet up time/ location

Area name/ Closest Town

Est. Duration

GPS / Latitude & Longitude / Grid Ref

Est. Distance   Km   Miles

Loop / Line & Back / One Way   Day Trip / Overnight/ Holiday

Local Contact

Accommodation Info

THE EQUIPMENT

A   B

Map Name/No

THE HIKE

(M) (P)

Start Time

End Time

Actual Distance

Total No of Steps

Calories Burned

POINTS OF INTEREST

Difficulty Level (1 Easy 5 Hard) △

Enjoyment Level (1 Bad 5 Good) ♡

Overall Grade (1 Bad 5 Good) ☆

Notes
Facilities
Parking
Costs
Nature
Etc

MY MUNRO TOTAL

THE PLAN

Date

MUNRO NAME	My Ref

Meet up time/ location

Area name/ Closest Town

Est. Duration

GPS / Latitude & Longitude / Grid Ref

Est. Distance _____ Km / Miles

Loop / Line & Back / One Way   Day Trip / Overnight/ Holiday

Local Contact

Accommodation Info

THE EQUIPMENT

A   B

Map Name/No

THE HIKE

(M) (P)

Start Time

End Time

Actual Distance

Total No of Steps

Calories Burned

POINTS OF INTEREST

Difficulty Level (1 Easy 5 Hard)   △

Enjoyment Level (1 Bad 5 Good)   ♡

Overall Grade (1 Bad 5 Good)   ☆

Notes
Facilities
Parking
Costs
Nature
Etc

MY MUNRO TOTAL

THE PLAN

MUNRO NAME

My Ref

Date

Meet up time/ location

Area name/ Closest Town

Est. Duration

GPS / Latitude & Longitude / Grid Ref

Est. Distance

Km
Miles

Loop / Line & Back / One Way   Day Trip / Overnight/ Holiday

Local Contact

Accommodation Info

THE EQUIPMENT

A   B

Map Name/No

THE HIKE

Start Time

End Time

M   P

Actual Distance

Total No of Steps

Calories
Burned

POINTS OF INTEREST

Difficulty Level (1 Easy 5 Hard)

Enjoyment Level (1 Bad 5 Good)

Overall Grade (1 Bad 5 Good)

Notes
Facilities
Parking
Costs
Nature
Etc

MY MUNRO TOTAL

THE PLAN

Date

MUNRO NAME

My Ref .

Meet up time/ location	Area name/ Closest Town
Est. Duration	GPS / Latitude & Longitude / Grid Ref
Est. Distance Km Miles	
	Loop / Line & Back / One Way Day Trip / Overnight/ Holiday
Local Contact	Accommodation Info

THE EQUIPMENT

A   B

Map Name/No

THE HIKE

POINTS OF INTEREST

Start Time

End Time

Actual Distance

Total No of Steps

Calories Burned

Difficulty Level (1 Easy 5 Hard) △

Enjoyment Level (1 Bad 5 Good) ♡

Overall Grade (1 Bad 5 Good) ☆

Notes
Facilities
Parking
Costs
Nature
Etc

MY MUNRO TOTAL

THE PLAN

MUNRO NAME

My Ref

Date

Meet up time/ location

Area name/ Closest Town

Est. Duration

GPS / Latitude & Longitude / Grid Ref

Est. Distance

Km
Miles

Loop / Line & Back / One Way   Day Trip / Overnight/ Holiday

Local Contact

Accommodation Info

THE EQUIPMENT

A   B

Map Name/No

THE HIKE

Start Time

End Time

Actual Distance

Total No of Steps

Calories
Burned

(M) (P)

POINTS OF INTEREST

Difficulty Level (1 Easy 5 Hard) △

Enjoyment Level (1 Bad 5 Good) ♡

Overall Grade (1 Bad 5 Good) ☆

Notes
Facilities
Parking
Costs
Nature
Etc

MY MUNRO TOTAL

THE PLAN

Date

MUNRO NAME

My Ref

Meet up time/ location

Area name/ Closest Town

Est. Duration

GPS / Latitude & Longitude / Grid Ref

Est. Distance

Km
Miles

Local Contact

Loop / Line & Back / One Way   Day Trip / Overnight/ Holiday

Accommodation Info

THE EQUIPMENT

A   B

Map Name/No

THE HIKE

(M) (P)

Start Time

End Time

Actual Distance

Total No of Steps

Calories
Burned

POINTS OF INTEREST

Difficulty Level (1 Easy 5 Hard) △

Enjoyment Level (1 Bad 5 Good) ♡

Overall Grade (1 Bad 5 Good) ☆

Notes
Facilities
Parking
Costs
Nature
Etc

MY MUNRO TOTAL

THE PLAN

Date	MUNRO NAME
	My Ref

Meet up time/ location | Area name/ Closest Town

Est. Duration | GPS / Latitude & Longitude / Grid Ref

Est. Distance   Km Miles |

Loop / Line & Back / One Way   Day Trip / Overnight/ Holiday

Local Contact | Accommodation Info

THE EQUIPMENT

A   B

Map Name/No

THE HIKE

Start Time

End Time

Actual Distance

Total No of Steps

M   P

POINTS OF INTEREST

Calories Burned

Difficulty Level (1 Easy 5 Hard) △

Enjoyment Level (1 Bad 5 Good) ♡

Overall Grade (1 Bad 5 Good) ☆

Notes
Facilities
Parking
Costs
Nature
Etc

MY MUNRO TOTAL

THE PLAN

Date

MUNRO NAME

My Ref

Meet up time/ location

Area name/ Closest Town

Est. Duration

GPS / Latitude & Longitude / Grid Ref

Est. Distance

Km
Miles

Loop / Line & Back / One Way   Day Trip / Overnight/ Holiday

Local Contact

Accommodation Info

THE EQUIPMENT

A   B

Map Name/No

THE HIKE

M   P

Start Time

End Time

Actual Distance

Total No of Steps

Calories
Burned

POINTS OF INTEREST

Difficulty Level (1 Easy 5 Hard)

Enjoyment Level (1 Bad 5 Good)

Overall Grade (1 Bad 5 Good)

Notes
Facilities
Parking
Costs
Nature
Etc

MY MUNRO TOTAL

THE PLAN

Date

	MUNRO NAME	My Ref

Meet up time/ location

Area name/ Closest Town

Est. Duration

GPS / Latitude & Longitude / Grid Ref

Est. Distance

Km
Miles

Loop / Line & Back / One Way   Day Trip / Overnight/ Holiday

Local Contact

Accommodation Info

THE EQUIPMENT

A   B

Map Name/No

THE HIKE

(M)   (P)

Start Time

End Time

Actual Distance

Total No of Steps

Calories
Burned

POINTS OF INTEREST

Difficulty Level (1 Easy 5 Hard) △

Enjoyment Level (1 Bad 5 Good) ♡

Overall Grade (1 Bad 5 Good) ☆

Notes
Facilities
Parking
Costs
Nature
Etc

MY MUNRO TOTAL

THE PLAN

Date

MUNRO NAME

My Ref

Meet up time/ location

Area name/ Closest Town

Est. Duration

GPS / Latitude & Longitude / Grid Ref

Est. Distance

Km
Miles

Loop / Line & Back / One Way   Day Trip / Overnight/ Holiday

Local Contact

Accommodation Info

THE EQUIPMENT

A   B

Map Name/No

THE HIKE

Start Time

End Time

Actual Distance

Total No of Steps

Calories
Burned

(M) (P)

POINTS OF INTEREST

Difficulty Level (1 Easy 5 Hard)

Enjoyment Level (1 Bad 5 Good)

Overall Grade (1 Bad 5 Good)

Notes
Facilities
Parking
Costs
Nature
Etc

MY MUNRO TOTAL

THE PLAN

	MUNRO NAME	My Ref
Date		

Meet up time/ location

Area name/ Closest Town

Est. Duration

GPS / Latitude & Longitude / Grid Ref

Est. Distance
Km
Miles

Loop / Line & Back / One Way   Day Trip / Overnight/ Holiday

Local Contact

Accommodation Info

THE EQUIPMENT

A   B

Map Name/No

THE HIKE

(M) (P)

Start Time

End Time

Actual Distance

Total No of Steps

Calories Burned

POINTS OF INTEREST

Difficulty Level (1 Easy 5 Hard) △

Enjoyment Level (1 Bad 5 Good) ♡

Overall Grade (1 Bad 5 Good) ☆

Notes
Facilities
Parking
Costs
Nature
Etc

MY MUNRO TOTAL

THE PLAN

Date

| MUNRO NAME | My Ref |

Meet up time/ location

Area name/ Closest Town

Est. Duration

GPS / Latitude & Longitude / Grid Ref

Est. Distance

Km
Miles

Loop / Line & Back / One Way   Day Trip / Overnight/ Holiday

Local Contact

Accommodation Info

THE EQUIPMENT

A   B

Map Name/No

THE HIKE

Start Time

End Time

(M) (P)

Actual Distance

Total No of Steps

Calories
Burned

POINTS OF INTEREST

Difficulty Level (1 Easy 5 Hard) △

Enjoyment Level (1 Bad 5 Good) ♡

Overall Grade (1 Bad 5 Good) ☆

Notes
Facilities
Parking
Costs
Nature
Etc

MY MUNRO TOTAL

THE PLAN

Date

MUNRO NAME

My Ref

Meet up time/ location

Area name/ Closest Town

Est. Duration

GPS / Latitude & Longitude / Grid Ref

Est. Distance

Km
Miles

Loop / Line & Back / One Way   Day Trip / Overnight/ Holiday

Local Contact

Accommodation Info

THE EQUIPMENT

A   B

Map Name/No

THE HIKE

Start Time

End Time

M   P

Actual Distance

Total No of Steps

Calories
Burned

POINTS OF INTEREST

Difficulty Level (1 Easy 5 Hard)

Enjoyment Level (1 Bad 5 Good)

Overall Grade (1 Bad 5 Good)

Notes
Facilities
Parking
Costs
Nature
Etc

MY MUNRO TOTAL

THE PLAN

Date

MUNRO NAME	My Ref

Meet up time/ location

Area name/ Closest Town

Est. Duration

GPS / Latitude & Longitude / Grid Ref

Est. Distance

Km
Miles

Loop / Line & Back / One Way   Day Trip / Overnight/ Holiday

Local Contact

Accommodation Info

THE EQUIPMENT

A B

Map Name/No

THE HIKE

M   P

Start Time

End Time

Actual Distance

Total No of Steps

Calories
Burned

POINTS OF INTEREST

Difficulty Level (1 Easy 5 Hard)

Enjoyment Level (1 Bad 5 Good)

Overall Grade (1 Bad 5 Good)

Notes
Facilities
Parking
Costs
Nature
Etc

MY MUNRO TOTAL

THE PLAN

	MUNRO NAME	My Ref
Date		

Meet up time/ location	Area name/ Closest Town
Est. Duration	GPS / Latitude & Longitude / Grid Ref
Est. Distance Km Miles	
	Loop / Line & Back / One Way Day Trip / Overnight/ Holiday
Local Contact	Accommodation Info

THE EQUIPMENT

A   B

Map Name/No

THE HIKE

M   P

Start Time

End Time

Actual Distance

Total No of Steps

Calories Burned

POINTS OF INTEREST

Difficulty Level (1 Easy 5 Hard) △

Enjoyment Level (1 Bad 5 Good) ♡

Overall Grade (1 Bad 5 Good) ☆

Notes
Facilities
Parking
Costs
Nature
Etc

MY MUNRO TOTAL

THE PLAN

Date

MUNRO NAME

My Ref

Meet up time/ location

Area name/ Closest Town

Est. Duration

GPS / Latitude & Longitude / Grid Ref

Est. Distance

Km
Miles

Local Contact

Loop / Line & Back / One Way   Day Trip / Overnight/ Holiday

Accommodation Info

THE EQUIPMENT

A   B

Map Name/No

THE HIKE

Start Time

End Time

Actual Distance

Total No of Steps

M   P

POINTS OF INTEREST

Calories
Burned

Difficulty Level (1 Easy 5 Hard) △

Enjoyment Level (1 Bad 5 Good) ♡

Overall Grade (1 Bad 5 Good) ☆

Notes
Facilities
Parking
Costs
Nature
Etc

MY MUNRO TOTAL

THE PLAN

Date

MUNRO NAME

My Ref

Meet up time/ location

Area name/ Closest Town

Est. Duration

GPS / Latitude & Longitude / Grid Ref

Est. Distance   Km
                                 Miles

Loop / Line & Back / One Way   Day Trip / Overnight/ Holiday

Local Contact

Accommodation Info

THE EQUIPMENT

A   B

Map Name/No

THE HIKE

(M) (P)

Start Time

End Time

Actual Distance

Total No of Steps

Calories
Burned

POINTS OF INTEREST

Difficulty Level (1 Easy 5 Hard) △

Enjoyment Level (1 Bad 5 Good) ♡

Overall Grade (1 Bad 5 Good) ☆

Notes
Facilities
Parking
Costs
Nature
Etc

MY MUNRO TOTAL

THE PLAN

MUNRO NAME

My Ref

Date

Meet up time/ location

Area name/ Closest Town

Est. Duration

GPS / Latitude & Longitude / Grid Ref

Est. Distance

Km
Miles

Loop / Line & Back / One Way   Day Trip / Overnight/ Holiday

Local Contact

Accommodation Info

THE EQUIPMENT

A   B

Map Name/No

THE HIKE

Start Time

End Time

(M) (P)

Actual Distance

Total No of Steps

Calories
Burned

POINTS OF INTEREST

Difficulty Level (1 Easy 5 Hard)

Enjoyment Level (1 Bad 5 Good)

Overall Grade (1 Bad 5 Good)

Notes
Facilities
Parking
Costs
Nature
Etc

MY MUNRO TOTAL

THE PLAN

Date

MUNRO NAME

My Ref

Meet up time/ location	Area name/ Closest Town
Est. Duration	GPS / Latitude & Longitude / Grid Ref
Est. Distance _Km Miles_	Loop / Line & Back / One Way Day Trip / Overnight/ Holiday
Local Contact	Accommodation Info

THE EQUIPMENT

A B

Map Name/No

THE HIKE

Start Time

End Time

M P

Actual Distance

Total No of Steps

Calories Burned

POINTS OF INTEREST

Difficulty Level (1 Easy 5 Hard) △

Enjoyment Level (1 Bad 5 Good) ♡

Overall Grade (1 Bad 5 Good) ☆

Notes
Facilities
Parking
Costs
Nature
Etc

MY MUNRO TOTAL

THE PLAN

Date

MUNRO NAME

My Ref

Meet up time/ location

Area name/ Closest Town

Est. Duration

GPS / Latitude & Longitude / Grid Ref

Est. Distance

Km
Miles

Loop / Line & Back / One Way   Day Trip / Overnight/ Holiday

Local Contact

Accommodation Info

THE EQUIPMENT

A   B

Map Name/No

THE HIKE

Start Time

End Time

Actual Distance

Total No of Steps

Calories
Burned

M   P

POINTS OF INTEREST

Difficulty Level (1 Easy 5 Hard)

Enjoyment Level (1 Bad 5 Good)

Overall Grade (1 Bad 5 Good)

Notes
Facilities
Parking
Costs
Nature
Etc

MY MUNRO TOTAL

THE PLAN

Date

MUNRO NAME	My Ref

Meet up time/ location

Area name/ Closest Town

Est. Duration

GPS / Latitude & Longitude / Grid Ref

Est. Distance   Km
                       Miles

Loop / Line & Back / One Way   Day Trip / Overnight/ Holiday

Local Contact

Accommodation Info

THE EQUIPMENT

A   B

Map Name/No

THE HIKE

(M) (P)

Start Time

End Time

Actual Distance

Total No of Steps

Calories
Burned

POINTS OF INTEREST

Difficulty Level (1 Easy 5 Hard) △

Enjoyment Level (1 Bad 5 Good) ♡

Overall Grade (1 Bad 5 Good) ☆

Notes
Facilities
Parking
Costs
Nature
Etc

MY MUNRO TOTAL

THE PLAN

Date

| MUNRO NAME | | My Ref |

Meet up time/ location

Area name/ Closest Town

Est. Duration

GPS / Latitude & Longitude / Grid Ref

Est. Distance   Km
                                 Miles

Loop / Line & Back / One Way   Day Trip / Overnight/ Holiday

Local Contact

Accommodation Info

THE EQUIPMENT

A   B

Map Name/No

THE HIKE

Start Time

End Time

Actual Distance

Total No of Steps

(M) (P)

POINTS OF INTEREST

Calories
Burned

Difficulty Level (1 Easy 5 Hard) △

Enjoyment Level (1 Bad 5 Good) ♡

Overall Grade (1 Bad 5 Good) ☆

Notes
Facilities
Parking
Costs
Nature
Etc

MY MUNRO TOTAL

THE PLAN

Date

MUNRO NAME	My Ref

Meet up time/ location

Area name/ Closest Town

Est. Duration

GPS / Latitude & Longitude / Grid Ref

Est. Distance
Km
Miles

Loop / Line & Back / One Way   Day Trip / Overnight/ Holiday

Local Contact

Accommodation Info

THE EQUIPMENT

A   B

Map Name/No

THE HIKE

(M) (P)

Start Time

End Time

Actual Distance

Total No of Steps

Calories
Burned

POINTS OF INTEREST

Difficulty Level (1 Easy 5 Hard) △

Enjoyment Level (1 Bad 5 Good) ♡

Overall Grade (1 Bad 5 Good) ☆

Notes
Facilities
Parking
Costs
Nature
Etc

MY MUNRO TOTAL

THE PLAN

Date

MUNRO NAME

My Ref

Meet up time/ location

Area name/ Closest Town

Est. Duration

GPS / Latitude & Longitude / Grid Ref

Est. Distance

Km
Miles

Loop / Line & Back / One Way   Day Trip / Overnight/ Holiday

Local Contact

Accommodation Info

THE EQUIPMENT

A   B

Map Name/No

THE HIKE

(M) (P)

Start Time

End Time

Actual Distance

Total No of Steps

Calories
Burned

POINTS OF INTEREST

Difficulty Level (1 Easy 5 Hard) △

Enjoyment Level (1 Bad 5 Good) ♡

Overall Grade (1 Bad 5 Good) ☆

Notes
Facilities
Parking
Costs
Nature
Etc

MY MUNRO TOTAL

THE PLAN

MUNRO NAME

My Ref

Date

Meet up time/ location

Area name/ Closest Town

Est. Duration

GPS / Latitude & Longitude / Grid Ref

Est. Distance

Km
Miles

Loop / Line & Back / One Way   Day Trip / Overnight/ Holiday

Local Contact

Accommodation Info

THE EQUIPMENT

A   B

Map Name/No

THE HIKE

Start Time

End Time

Actual Distance

M   P

Total No of Steps

Calories
Burned

POINTS OF INTEREST

Difficulty Level (1 Easy 5 Hard) △

Enjoyment Level (1 Bad 5 Good) ♡

Overall Grade (1 Bad 5 Good) ☆

Notes
Facilities
Parking
Costs
Nature
Etc

MY MUNRO TOTAL

THE PLAN

Date

MUNRO NAME	My Ref

Meet up time/ location

Area name/ Closest Town

Est. Duration

GPS / Latitude & Longitude / Grid Ref

Est. Distance   Km
                                 Miles

Loop / Line & Back / One Way   Day Trip / Overnight/ Holiday

Local Contact

Accommodation Info

THE EQUIPMENT

A   B

Map Name/No

THE HIKE

M   P

POINTS OF INTEREST

Start Time

End Time

Actual Distance

Total No of Steps

Calories
Burned

Difficulty Level (1 Easy 5 Hard) △

Enjoyment Level (1 Bad 5 Good) ♡

Overall Grade (1 Bad 5 Good) ☆

Notes
Facilities
Parking
Costs
Nature
Etc

MY MUNRO TOTAL

THE PLAN

Date

MUNRO NAME

My Ref

Meet up time/ location	Area name/ Closest Town
Est. Duration	GPS / Latitude & Longitude / Grid Ref
Est. Distance _____ Km Miles	Loop / Line & Back / One Way Day Trip / Overnight/ Holiday
Local Contact	Accommodation Info

THE EQUIPMENT

A B

Map Name/No

THE HIKE

M   P

Start Time

End Time

Actual Distance

Total No of Steps

Calories Burned

POINTS OF INTEREST

Difficulty Level (1 Easy 5 Hard) △

Enjoyment Level (1 Bad 5 Good) ♡

Overall Grade (1 Bad 5 Good) ☆

Notes
Facilities
Parking
Costs
Nature
Etc

MY MUNRO TOTAL

THE PLAN

Date

MUNRO NAME

My Ref

Meet up time/ location

Area name/ Closest Town

Est. Duration

GPS / Latitude & Longitude / Grid Ref

Est. Distance

Km
Miles

Loop / Line & Back / One Way   Day Trip / Overnight/ Holiday

Local Contact

Accommodation Info

THE EQUIPMENT

A   B

Map Name/No

THE HIKE

Start Time

End Time

M   P

Actual Distance

Total No of Steps

POINTS OF INTEREST

Calories
Burned

Difficulty Level (1 Easy 5 Hard)

Enjoyment Level (1 Bad 5 Good)

Overall Grade (1 Bad 5 Good)

Notes
Facilities
Parking
Costs
Nature
Etc

MY MUNRO TOTAL

THE PLAN

MUNRO NAME

My Ref

Date

Meet up time/ location	Area name/ Closest Town
Est. Duration	GPS / Latitude & Longitude / Grid Ref
Est. Distance Km Miles	Loop / Line & Back / One Way Day Trip / Overnight/ Holiday
Local Contact	Accommodation Info

THE EQUIPMENT

A   B

Map Name/No

THE HIKE

Start Time

End Time

Actual Distance

Total No of Steps

Calories Burned

POINTS OF INTEREST

Difficulty Level (1 Easy 5 Hard) △

Enjoyment Level (1 Bad 5 Good) ♡

Overall Grade (1 Bad 5 Good) ☆

Notes
Facilities
Parking
Costs
Nature
Etc

MY MUNRO TOTAL

THE PLAN

Date

MUNRO NAME

My Ref

Meet up time/ location

Area name/ Closest Town

Est. Duration

GPS / Latitude & Longitude / Grid Ref

Est. Distance

Km
Miles

Loop / Line & Back / One Way   Day Trip / Overnight/ Holiday

Local Contact

Accommodation Info

THE EQUIPMENT

A   B

Map Name/No

THE HIKE

M   P

Start Time

End Time

Actual Distance

Total No of Steps

Calories
Burned

POINTS OF INTEREST

Difficulty Level (1 Easy 5 Hard) △

Enjoyment Level (1 Bad 5 Good) ♡

Overall Grade (1 Bad 5 Good) ☆

Notes
Facilities
Parking
Costs
Nature
Etc

MY MUNRO TOTAL

THE PLAN

	MUNRO NAME	My Ref

Date

Meet up time/ location	Area name/ Closest Town
Est. Duration	GPS / Latitude & Longitude / Grid Ref
Est. Distance Km Miles	Loop / Line & Back / One Way Day Trip / Overnight/ Holiday
Local Contact	Accommodation Info

THE EQUIPMENT

A   B

Map Name/No

THE HIKE

M   P

Start Time

End Time

Actual Distance

Total No of Steps

Calories Burned

POINTS OF INTEREST

Difficulty Level (1 Easy 5 Hard) △

Enjoyment Level (1 Bad 5 Good) ♡

Overall Grade (1 Bad 5 Good) ☆

Notes
Facilities
Parking
Costs
Nature
Etc

MY MUNRO TOTAL

THE PLAN

Date

MUNRO NAME

My Ref

Meet up time/ location

Area name/ Closest Town

Est. Duration

GPS / Latitude & Longitude / Grid Ref

Est. Distance

Km
Miles

Loop / Line & Back / One Way   Day Trip / Overnight/ Holiday

Local Contact

Accommodation Info

THE EQUIPMENT

A   B

Map Name/No

THE HIKE

Start Time

End Time

(M) (P)

Actual Distance

Total No of Steps

Calories
Burned

POINTS OF INTEREST

Difficulty Level (1 Easy 5 Hard) △

Enjoyment Level (1 Bad 5 Good) ♡

Overall Grade (1 Bad 5 Good) ☆

Notes
Facilities
Parking
Costs
Nature
Etc

MY MUNRO TOTAL

THE PLAN

MUNRO NAME

My Ref

Date

Meet up time/ location

Est. Duration

Est. Distance
Km
Miles

Local Contact

Area name/ Closest Town

GPS / Latitude & Longitude / Grid Ref

Loop / Line & Back / One Way   Day Trip / Overnight/ Holiday

Accommodation Info

THE EQUIPMENT

A   B

Map Name/No

THE HIKE

(M)   (P)

Start Time

End Time

Actual Distance

Total No of Steps

Calories
Burned

POINTS OF INTEREST

Difficulty Level (1 Easy 5 Hard) △

Enjoyment Level (1 Bad 5 Good) ♡

Overall Grade (1 Bad 5 Good) ☆

Notes
Facilities
Parking
Costs
Nature
Etc

MY MUNRO TOTAL

THE PLAN

Date

Meet up time/ location

Est. Duration

Est. Distance

Km
Miles

Local Contact

MUNRO NAME

My Ref

Area name/ Closest Town

GPS / Latitude & Longitude / Grid Ref

Loop / Line & Back / One Way   Day Trip / Overnight/ Holiday

Accommodation Info

THE EQUIPMENT

A   B

Map Name/No

THE HIKE

M   P

Start Time

End Time

Actual Distance

Total No of Steps

POINTS OF INTEREST

Calories
Burned

Difficulty Level (1 Easy 5 Hard) △

Enjoyment Level (1 Bad 5 Good) ♡

Overall Grade (1 Bad 5 Good) ☆

Notes
Facilities
Parking
Costs
Nature
Etc

MY MUNRO TOTAL

THE PLAN

Date

MUNRO NAME

My Ref

Meet up time/ location

Area name/ Closest Town

Est. Duration

GPS / Latitude & Longitude / Grid Ref

Est. Distance   Km
                       Miles

Loop / Line & Back / One Way   Day Trip / Overnight/ Holiday

Local Contact

Accommodation Info

THE EQUIPMENT

A   B

Map Name/No

THE HIKE

Start Time

End Time

Actual Distance

Total No of Steps

Calories
Burned

POINTS OF INTEREST

Difficulty Level (1 Easy 5 Hard) △

Enjoyment Level (1 Bad 5 Good) ♡

Overall Grade (1 Bad 5 Good) ☆

Notes
Facilities
Parking
Costs
Nature
Etc

MY MUNRO TOTAL

THE PLAN

Date

MUNRO NAME

My Ref

| Meet up time/ location | Area name/ Closest Town |

Est. Duration | GPS / Latitude & Longitude / Grid Ref

Est. Distance

Km
Miles

Loop / Line & Back / One Way   Day Trip / Overnight/ Holiday

Local Contact | Accommodation Info

THE EQUIPMENT

A   B

Map Name/No

THE HIKE

Start Time

End Time

Actual Distance

Total No of Steps

M   P

POINTS OF INTEREST

Calories
Burned

Difficulty Level (1 Easy 5 Hard) △

Enjoyment Level (1 Bad 5 Good) ♡

Overall Grade (1 Bad 5 Good) ☆

Notes
Facilities
Parking
Costs
Nature
Etc

MY MUNRO TOTAL

THE PLAN

Date

| MUNRO NAME | My Ref |

Meet up time/ location

Area name/ Closest Town

Est. Duration

GPS / Latitude & Longitude / Grid Ref

Est. Distance   Km
                                        Miles

Loop / Line & Back / One Way   Day Trip / Overnight/ Holiday

Local Contact

Accommodation Info

THE EQUIPMENT

A   B

Map Name/No

THE HIKE

(M) (P)

Start Time

End Time

Actual Distance

Total No of Steps

Calories
Burned

POINTS OF INTEREST

Difficulty Level (1 Easy 5 Hard) △

Enjoyment Level (1 Bad 5 Good) ♡

Overall Grade (1 Bad 5 Good) ☆

Notes
Facilities
Parking
Costs
Nature
Etc

MY MUNRO TOTAL

THE PLAN

Date

MUNRO NAME	My Ref

Meet up time/ location

Area name/ Closest Town

Est. Duration

GPS / Latitude & Longitude / Grid Ref

Est. Distance

Km
Miles

Loop / Line & Back / One Way   Day Trip / Overnight/ Holiday

Local Contact

Accommodation Info

THE EQUIPMENT

A   B

Map Name/No

THE HIKE

M   P

Start Time

End Time

Actual Distance

Total No of Steps

Calories
Burned

POINTS OF INTEREST

Difficulty Level (1 Easy 5 Hard) △

Enjoyment Level (1 Bad 5 Good) ♡

Overall Grade (1 Bad 5 Good) ☆

Notes
Facilities
Parking
Costs
Nature
Etc

MY MUNRO TOTAL

THE PLAN

MUNRO NAME

My Ref

Date

Meet up time/ location

Area name/ Closest Town

Est. Duration

GPS / Latitude & Longitude / Grid Ref

Est. Distance

Km
Miles

Loop / Line & Back / One Way   Day Trip / Overnight/ Holiday

Local Contact

Accommodation Info

THE EQUIPMENT

A   B

Map Name/No

THE HIKE

Start Time

End Time

M   P

Actual Distance

Total No of Steps

Calories
Burned

POINTS OF INTEREST

Difficulty Level (1 Easy 5 Hard)

Enjoyment Level (1 Bad 5 Good)

Overall Grade (1 Bad 5 Good)

Notes
Facilities
Parking
Costs
Nature
Etc

MY MUNRO TOTAL

THE PLAN

Date

MUNRO NAME

My Ref

Meet up time/ location

Area name/ Closest Town

Est. Duration

GPS / Latitude & Longitude / Grid Ref

Est. Distance

Km
Miles

Loop / Line & Back / One Way   Day Trip / Overnight/ Holiday

Local Contact

Accommodation Info

THE EQUIPMENT

A   B

Map Name/No

THE HIKE

M   P

Start Time

End Time

Actual Distance

Total No of Steps

POINTS OF INTEREST

Calories
Burned

Difficulty Level (1 Easy 5 Hard)

Enjoyment Level (1 Bad 5 Good)

Overall Grade (1 Bad 5 Good)

Notes
Facilities
Parking
Costs
Nature
Etc

MY MUNRO TOTAL

THE PLAN

Date

	MUNRO NAME	My Ref

Meet up time/ location

Area name/ Closest Town

Est. Duration

GPS / Latitude & Longitude / Grid Ref

Est. Distance   Km
                       Miles

Loop / Line & Back / One Way   Day Trip / Overnight/ Holiday

Local Contact

Accommodation Info

THE EQUIPMENT

A   B

Map Name/No

THE HIKE

Start Time

End Time

Actual Distance

Total No of Steps

Calories Burned

(M)   (P)

POINTS OF INTEREST

Difficulty Level (1 Easy 5 Hard) △

Enjoyment Level (1 Bad 5 Good) ♡

Overall Grade (1 Bad 5 Good) ☆

Notes
Facilities
Parking
Costs
Nature
Etc

MY MUNRO TOTAL

THE PLAN

THE PLAN Date	MUNRO NAME	My Ref
Meet up time/ location	Area name/ Closest Town	
Est. Duration	GPS / Latitude & Longitude / Grid Ref	
Est. Distance Km Miles	Loop / Line & Back / One Way Day Trip / Overnight/ Holiday	
Local Contact	Accommodation Info	

THE EQUIPMENT

A   B

Map Name/No

THE HIKE

Start Time

End Time

Actual Distance

Total No of Steps

(M) (P)

POINTS OF INTEREST

Calories Burned

Difficulty Level (1 Easy 5 Hard) △

Enjoyment Level (1 Bad 5 Good) ♡

Overall Grade (1 Bad 5 Good) ☆

Notes
Facilities
Parking
Costs
Nature
Etc

MY MUNRO TOTAL

THE PLAN

Date

MUNRO NAME	My Ref

Meet up time/ location

Area name/ Closest Town

Est. Duration

GPS / Latitude & Longitude / Grid Ref

Est. Distance   Km
                       Miles

Loop / Line & Back / One Way   Day Trip / Overnight/ Holiday

Local Contact

Accommodation Info

THE EQUIPMENT

A   B

Map Name/No

THE HIKE

Start Time

End Time

Actual Distance

Total No of Steps

M   P

POINTS OF INTEREST

Calories
Burned

Difficulty Level (1 Easy 5 Hard)

Enjoyment Level (1 Bad 5 Good)

Overall Grade (1 Bad 5 Good)

Notes
Facilities
Parking
Costs
Nature
Etc

MY MUNRO TOTAL

THE PLAN

Date

MUNRO NAME

My Ref

Meet up time/ location

Area name/ Closest Town

Est. Duration

GPS / Latitude & Longitude / Grid Ref

Est. Distance   Km
                      Miles

Loop / Line & Back / One Way   Day Trip / Overnight/ Holiday

Local Contact

Accommodation Info

THE EQUIPMENT

A   B

Map Name/No

THE HIKE

Start Time

End Time

Actual Distance

Total No of Steps

Calories
Burned

POINTS OF INTEREST

Difficulty Level (1 Easy 5 Hard) △

Enjoyment Level (1 Bad 5 Good) ♡

Overall Grade (1 Bad 5 Good) ☆

Notes
Facilities
Parking
Costs
Nature
Etc

MY MUNRO TOTAL

THE PLAN

Date

	MUNRO NAME	My Ref

Meet up time/ location

Est. Duration

Est. Distance   Km / Miles

Local Contact

Area name/ Closest Town

GPS / Latitude & Longitude / Grid Ref

Loop / Line & Back / One Way   Day Trip / Overnight/ Holiday

Accommodation Info

THE EQUIPMENT

A   B

Map Name/No

THE HIKE

Start Time

End Time

Actual Distance

Total No of Steps

POINTS OF INTEREST

Calories Burned

Difficulty Level (1 Easy 5 Hard) △

Enjoyment Level (1 Bad 5 Good) ♡

Overall Grade (1 Bad 5 Good) ☆

Notes
Facilities
Parking
Costs
Nature
Etc

MY MUNRO TOTAL

THE PLAN

	MUNRO NAME	My Ref
Date		

Meet up time/ location

Area name/ Closest Town

Est. Duration

GPS / Latitude & Longitude / Grid Ref

Est. Distance

Km
Miles

Loop / Line & Back / One Way   Day Trip / Overnight/ Holiday

Local Contact

Accommodation Info

THE EQUIPMENT

A   B

Map Name/No

THE HIKE

Start Time

End Time

Actual Distance

(M) (P)

Total No of Steps

Calories
Burned

POINTS OF INTEREST

Difficulty Level (1 Easy 5 Hard) △

Enjoyment Level (1 Bad 5 Good) ♡

Overall Grade (1 Bad 5 Good) ☆

Notes
Facilities
Parking
Costs
Nature
Etc

MY MUNRO TOTAL

THE PLAN

Date	

MUNRO NAME

My Ref

Meet up time/ location

Area name/ Closest Town

Est. Duration

GPS / Latitude & Longitude / Grid Ref

Est. Distance   Km
                       Miles

Loop / Line & Back / One Way   Day Trip / Overnight/ Holiday

Local Contact

Accommodation Info

THE EQUIPMENT

A   B

Map Name/No

THE HIKE

Start Time

End Time

Actual Distance

Total No of Steps

(M) (P)

Calories
Burned

POINTS OF INTEREST

Difficulty Level (1 Easy 5 Hard) △

Enjoyment Level (1 Bad 5 Good) ♡

Overall Grade (1 Bad 5 Good) ☆

Notes
Facilities
Parking
Costs
Nature
Etc

MY MUNRO TOTAL

THE PLAN

THE PLAN	MUNRO NAME	My Ref
Date		

Meet up time/ location	Area name/ Closest Town
Est. Duration	GPS / Latitude & Longitude / Grid Ref
Est. Distance Km Miles	
	Loop / Line & Back / One Way Day Trip / Overnight/ Holiday
Local Contact	Accommodation Info

THE EQUIPMENT

A   B

Map Name/No

THE HIKE

M   P

Start Time

End Time

Actual Distance

Total No of Steps

POINTS OF INTEREST

Calories
Burned

Difficulty Level (1 Easy 5 Hard) △

Enjoyment Level (1 Bad 5 Good) ♡

Overall Grade (1 Bad 5 Good) ☆

Notes
Facilities
Parking
Costs
Nature
Etc

MY MUNRO TOTAL

THE PLAN

	MUNRO NAME	My Ref
Date		

Meet up time/ location

Area name/ Closest Town

Est. Duration

GPS / Latitude & Longitude / Grid Ref

Est. Distance   Km
                       Miles

Loop / Line & Back / One Way   Day Trip / Overnight/ Holiday

Local Contact

Accommodation Info

THE EQUIPMENT

A   B

Map Name/No

THE HIKE

POINTS OF INTEREST

Start Time

End Time

Actual Distance

Total No of Steps

Calories Burned

Difficulty Level (1 Easy 5 Hard) △

Enjoyment Level (1 Bad 5 Good) ♡

Overall Grade (1 Bad 5 Good) ☆

Notes
Facilities
Parking
Costs
Nature
Etc

MY MUNRO TOTAL

THE PLAN

MUNRO NAME

My Ref

Date

Meet up time/ location

Area name/ Closest Town

Est. Duration

GPS / Latitude & Longitude / Grid Ref

Est. Distance

Km
Miles

Loop / Line & Back / One Way   Day Trip / Overnight/ Holiday

Local Contact

Accommodation Info

THE EQUIPMENT

A   B

Map Name/No

THE HIKE

Start Time

End Time

Actual Distance

Total No of Steps

Calories
Burned

M   P

POINTS OF INTEREST

Difficulty Level (1 Easy 5 Hard)

Enjoyment Level (1 Bad 5 Good)

Overall Grade (1 Bad 5 Good)

Notes
Facilities
Parking
Costs
Nature
Etc

MY MUNRO TOTAL

THE PLAN

MUNRO NAME

My Ref

Date

Meet up time/ location

Area name/ Closest Town

Est. Duration

GPS / Latitude & Longitude / Grid Ref

Est. Distance

Km
Miles

Loop / Line & Back / One Way   Day Trip / Overnight/ Holiday

Local Contact

Accommodation Info

THE EQUIPMENT

A   B

Map Name/No

THE HIKE

(M) (P)

Start Time

End Time

Actual Distance

Total No of Steps

Calories
Burned

POINTS OF INTEREST

Difficulty Level (1 Easy 5 Hard) △

Enjoyment Level (1 Bad 5 Good) ♡

Overall Grade (1 Bad 5 Good) ☆

Notes
Facilities
Parking
Costs
Nature
Etc

MY MUNRO TOTAL

THE PLAN

Date

	MUNRO NAME	My Ref

Meet up time/ location

Area name/ Closest Town

Est. Duration

GPS / Latitude & Longitude / Grid Ref

Est. Distance

Km
Miles

Loop / Line & Back / One Way   Day Trip / Overnight/ Holiday

Local Contact

Accommodation Info

THE EQUIPMENT

A B

Map Name/No

THE HIKE

(M) (P)

Start Time

End Time

Actual Distance

Total No of Steps

Calories
Burned

POINTS OF INTEREST

Difficulty Level (1 Easy 5 Hard) △

Enjoyment Level (1 Bad 5 Good) ♡

Overall Grade (1 Bad 5 Good) ☆

Notes
Facilities
Parking
Costs
Nature
Etc

MY MUNRO TOTAL

THE PLAN

Date

MUNRO NAME

My Ref

Meet up time/ location

Area name/ Closest Town

Est. Duration

GPS / Latitude & Longitude / Grid Ref

Est. Distance

Km
Miles

Loop / Line & Back / One Way   Day Trip / Overnight/ Holiday

Local Contact

Accommodation Info

THE EQUIPMENT

A   B

Map Name/No

THE HIKE

Start Time

End Time

Actual Distance

Total No of Steps

Calories
Burned

(M) (P)

POINTS OF INTEREST

Difficulty Level (1 Easy 5 Hard) △

Enjoyment Level (1 Bad 5 Good) ♡

Overall Grade (1 Bad 5 Good) ☆

Notes
Facilities
Parking
Costs
Nature
Etc

MY MUNRO TOTAL

THE PLAN

Date

MUNRO NAME

My Ref

Meet up time/ location

Area name/ Closest Town

Est. Duration

GPS / Latitude & Longitude / Grid Ref

Est. Distance

Km
Miles

Loop / Line & Back / One Way   Day Trip / Overnight/ Holiday

Local Contact

Accommodation Info

THE EQUIPMENT

A   B

Map Name/No

THE HIKE

(M) (P)

Start Time

End Time

Actual Distance

Total No of Steps

Calories
Burned

POINTS OF INTEREST

Difficulty Level (1 Easy 5 Hard) △

Enjoyment Level (1 Bad 5 Good) ♡

Overall Grade (1 Bad 5 Good) ☆

Notes
Facilities
Parking
Costs
Nature
Etc

MY MUNRO TOTAL

THE PLAN

Date

	MUNRO NAME	My Ref

Meet up time/ location

Est. Duration

Est. Distance   Km
                       Miles

Local Contact

Area name/ Closest Town

GPS / Latitude & Longitude / Grid Ref

Loop / Line & Back / One Way   Day Trip / Overnight/ Holiday

Accommodation Info

THE EQUIPMENT

A   B

Map Name/No

THE HIKE

(M) (P)

Start Time

End Time

Actual Distance

Total No of Steps

Calories
Burned

POINTS OF INTEREST

Difficulty Level (1 Easy 5 Hard) △

Enjoyment Level (1 Bad 5 Good) ♡

Overall Grade (1 Bad 5 Good) ☆

Notes
Facilities
Parking
Costs
Nature
Etc

MY MUNRO TOTAL

THE PLAN

Date

| MUNRO NAME | My Ref |

Meet up time/ location

Area name/ Closest Town

Est. Duration

GPS / Latitude & Longitude / Grid Ref

Est. Distance

Km
Miles

Loop / Line & Back / One Way   Day Trip / Overnight/ Holiday

Local Contact

Accommodation Info

THE EQUIPMENT

A   B

Map Name/No

THE HIKE

Start Time

End Time

Actual Distance

Total No of Steps

Calories
Burned

M   P

POINTS OF INTEREST

Difficulty Level (1 Easy 5 Hard)

Enjoyment Level (1 Bad 5 Good)

Overall Grade (1 Bad 5 Good)

Notes
Facilities
Parking
Costs
Nature
Etc

MY MUNRO TOTAL

THE PLAN

Date

MUNRO NAME

My Ref

Meet up time/ location	Area name/ Closest Town

Est. Duration	GPS / Latitude & Longitude / Grid Ref

| Est. Distance | Km / Miles |

Loop / Line & Back / One Way   Day Trip / Overnight/ Holiday

Local Contact	Accommodation Info

THE EQUIPMENT

A   B

Map Name/No

THE HIKE

(M)   (P)

Start Time

End Time

Actual Distance

Total No of Steps

Calories Burned

POINTS OF INTEREST

Difficulty Level (1 Easy 5 Hard) △

Enjoyment Level (1 Bad 5 Good) ♡

Overall Grade (1 Bad 5 Good) ☆

Notes
Facilities
Parking
Costs
Nature
Etc

MY MUNRO TOTAL

THE PLAN

Date

MUNRO NAME

My Ref

Meet up time/ location

Area name/ Closest Town

Est. Duration

GPS / Latitude & Longitude / Grid Ref

Est. Distance

Km
Miles

Loop / Line & Back / One Way   Day Trip / Overnight/ Holiday

Local Contact

Accommodation Info

THE EQUIPMENT

A   B

Map Name/No

THE HIKE

Start Time

End Time

Actual Distance

M   P

Total No of Steps

POINTS OF INTEREST

Calories
Burned

Difficulty Level (1 Easy 5 Hard)

Enjoyment Level (1 Bad 5 Good)

Overall Grade (1 Bad 5 Good)

Notes
Facilities
Parking
Costs
Nature
Etc

MY MUNRO TOTAL

THE PLAN

Date

MUNRO NAME

My Ref

Meet up time/ location

Area name/ Closest Town

Est. Duration

GPS / Latitude & Longitude / Grid Ref

Est. Distance   Km
                       Miles

Loop / Line & Back / One Way   Day Trip / Overnight/ Holiday

Local Contact

Accommodation Info

THE EQUIPMENT

A   B

Map Name/No

THE HIKE

Start Time

End Time

Actual Distance

Total No of Steps

Calories
Burned

M   P

POINTS OF INTEREST

Difficulty Level (1 Easy 5 Hard) △

Enjoyment Level (1 Bad 5 Good) ♡

Overall Grade (1 Bad 5 Good) ☆

Notes
Facilities
Parking
Costs
Nature
Etc

MY MUNRO TOTAL

THE PLAN

Date

MUNRO NAME

My Ref

Meet up time/ location	Area name/ Closest Town
Est. Duration	GPS / Latitude & Longitude / Grid Ref
Est. Distance Km Miles	
	Loop / Line & Back / One Way Day Trip / Overnight/ Holiday
Local Contact	Accommodation Info

THE EQUIPMENT

A   B

Map Name/No

THE HIKE

M   P

Start Time

End Time

Actual Distance

Total No of Steps

Calories Burned

POINTS OF INTEREST

Difficulty Level (1 Easy 5 Hard) △

Enjoyment Level (1 Bad 5 Good) ♡

Overall Grade (1 Bad 5 Good) ☆

Notes
Facilities
Parking
Costs
Nature
Etc

MY MUNRO TOTAL

THE PLAN

MUNRO NAME

My Ref

Date

Meet up time/ location

Area name/ Closest Town

Est. Duration

GPS / Latitude & Longitude / Grid Ref

Est. Distance

Km
Miles

Loop / Line & Back / One Way   Day Trip / Overnight/ Holiday

Local Contact

Accommodation Info

THE EQUIPMENT

A B

Map Name/No

THE HIKE

Start Time

End Time

M   P

Actual Distance

Total No of Steps

Calories
Burned

POINTS OF INTEREST

Difficulty Level (1 Easy 5 Hard) △

Enjoyment Level (1 Bad 5 Good) ♡

Overall Grade (1 Bad 5 Good) ☆

Notes
Facilities
Parking
Costs
Nature
Etc

MY MUNRO TOTAL

THE PLAN

Date

MUNRO NAME

My Ref

Meet up time/ location	Area name/ Closest Town
Est. Duration	GPS / Latitude & Longitude / Grid Ref
Est. Distance Km Miles	Loop / Line & Back / One Way Day Trip / Overnight/ Holiday
Local Contact	Accommodation Info

THE EQUIPMENT

A B

Map Name/No

THE HIKE

M   P

Start Time

End Time

Actual Distance

Total No of Steps

Calories Burned

POINTS OF INTEREST

Difficulty Level (1 Easy 5 Hard) △

Enjoyment Level (1 Bad 5 Good) ♡

Overall Grade (1 Bad 5 Good) ☆

Notes
Facilities
Parking
Costs
Nature
Etc

MY MUNRO TOTAL

THE PLAN

MUNRO NAME

My Ref

Date

Meet up time/ location

Area name/ Closest Town

Est. Duration

GPS / Latitude & Longitude / Grid Ref

Est. Distance

Km
Miles

Loop / Line & Back / One Way   Day Trip / Overnight/ Holiday

Local Contact

Accommodation Info

THE EQUIPMENT

A   B

Map Name/No

THE HIKE

Start Time

End Time

Actual Distance

(M)   (P)

Total No of Steps

Calories
Burned

POINTS OF INTEREST

Difficulty Level (1 Easy 5 Hard) △

Enjoyment Level (1 Bad 5 Good) ♡

Overall Grade (1 Bad 5 Good) ☆

Notes
Facilities
Parking
Costs
Nature
Etc

MY MUNRO TOTAL

THE PLAN

THE PLAN	**MUNRO NAME**	**My Ref**
Date		

Meet up time/ location

Area name/ Closest Town

Est. Duration

GPS / Latitude & Longitude / Grid Ref

Est. Distance   Km
                     Miles

Loop / Line & Back / One Way   Day Trip / Overnight/ Holiday

Local Contact

Accommodation Info

THE EQUIPMENT

A   B

Map Name/No

THE HIKE

Start Time

End Time

Actual Distance

(M)   (P)

Total No of Steps

Calories Burned

POINTS OF INTEREST

Difficulty Level (1 Easy 5 Hard)   △

Enjoyment Level (1 Bad 5 Good)   ♡

Overall Grade (1 Bad 5 Good)   ☆

Notes
Facilities
Parking
Costs
Nature
Etc

MY MUNRO TOTAL

THE PLAN

Date

MUNRO NAME

My Ref

Meet up time/ location

Area name/ Closest Town

Est. Duration

GPS / Latitude & Longitude / Grid Ref

Est. Distance

Km
Miles

Loop / Line & Back / One Way   Day Trip / Overnight/ Holiday

Local Contact

Accommodation Info

THE EQUIPMENT

A   B

Map Name/No

THE HIKE

M   P

Start Time

End Time

Actual Distance

Total No of Steps

Calories
Burned

POINTS OF INTEREST

Difficulty Level (1 Easy 5 Hard) △

Enjoyment Level (1 Bad 5 Good) ♡

Overall Grade (1 Bad 5 Good) ☆

Notes
Facilities
Parking
Costs
Nature
Etc

MY MUNRO TOTAL

THE PLAN

Date

MUNRO NAME

My Ref

Meet up time/ location

Area name/ Closest Town

Est. Duration

GPS / Latitude & Longitude / Grid Ref

Est. Distance

Km
Miles

Loop / Line & Back / One Way   Day Trip / Overnight/ Holiday

Local Contact

Accommodation Info

THE EQUIPMENT

A   B

Map Name/No

THE HIKE

M   P

Start Time

End Time

Actual Distance

Total No of Steps

Calories
Burned

POINTS OF INTEREST

Difficulty Level (1 Easy 5 Hard) △

Enjoyment Level (1 Bad 5 Good) ♡

Overall Grade (1 Bad 5 Good) ☆

Notes
Facilities
Parking
Costs
Nature
Etc

MY MUNRO TOTAL

THE PLAN

Date

MUNRO NAME

My Ref

Meet up time/ location

Area name/ Closest Town

Est. Duration

GPS / Latitude & Longitude / Grid Ref

Est. Distance

Km
Miles

Loop / Line & Back / One Way   Day Trip / Overnight/ Holiday

Local Contact

Accommodation Info

THE EQUIPMENT

A   B

Map Name/No

THE HIKE

Start Time

End Time

M   P

Actual Distance

Total No of Steps

Calories
Burned

POINTS OF INTEREST

Difficulty Level (1 Easy 5 Hard) △

Enjoyment Level (1 Bad 5 Good) ♡

Overall Grade (1 Bad 5 Good) ☆

Notes
Facilities
Parking
Costs
Nature
Etc

MY MUNRO TOTAL

THE PLAN

Date

MUNRO NAME		My Ref

Meet up time/ location

Area name/ Closest Town

Est. Duration

GPS / Latitude & Longitude / Grid Ref

Est. Distance   Km
                                  Miles

Loop / Line & Back / One Way   Day Trip / Overnight/ Holiday

Local Contact

Accommodation Info

THE EQUIPMENT

A   B

Map Name/No

THE HIKE

(M) (P)

Start Time

End Time

Actual Distance

Total No of Steps

Calories
Burned

POINTS OF INTEREST

Difficulty Level (1 Easy 5 Hard) △

Enjoyment Level (1 Bad 5 Good) ♡

Overall Grade (1 Bad 5 Good) ☆

Notes
Facilities
Parking
Costs
Nature
Etc

MY MUNRO TOTAL

THE PLAN

Date

MUNRO NAME

My Ref

Meet up time/ location

Area name/ Closest Town

Est. Duration

GPS / Latitude & Longitude / Grid Ref

Est. Distance

Km
Miles

Loop / Line & Back / One Way   Day Trip / Overnight/ Holiday

Local Contact

Accommodation Info

THE EQUIPMENT

A   B

Map Name/No

THE HIKE

(M)   (P)

Start Time

End Time

Actual Distance

Total No of Steps

Calories
Burned

POINTS OF INTEREST

Difficulty Level (1 Easy 5 Hard) △

Enjoyment Level (1 Bad 5 Good) ♡

Overall Grade (1 Bad 5 Good) ☆

Notes
Facilities
Parking
Costs
Nature
Etc

MY MUNRO TOTAL

THE PLAN

Date

| MUNRO NAME | My Ref |

Meet up time/ location

Area name/ Closest Town

Est. Duration

GPS / Latitude & Longitude / Grid Ref

Est. Distance   Km
                       Miles

Loop / Line & Back / One Way   Day Trip / Overnight/ Holiday

Local Contact

Accommodation Info

THE EQUIPMENT

A   B

Map Name/No

THE HIKE

Start Time

End Time

Actual Distance

Total No of Steps

Calories Burned

M   P

POINTS OF INTEREST

Difficulty Level (1 Easy 5 Hard) △

Enjoyment Level (1 Bad 5 Good) ♡

Overall Grade (1 Bad 5 Good) ☆

Notes
Facilities
Parking
Costs
Nature
Etc

MY MUNRO TOTAL

THE PLAN

	MUNRO NAME	My Ref
Date		

Meet up time/ location	Area name/ Closest Town
Est. Duration	GPS / Latitude & Longitude / Grid Ref
Est. Distance Km Miles	
	Loop / Line & Back / One Way Day Trip / Overnight/ Holiday
Local Contact	Accommodation Info

THE EQUIPMENT

A   B

Map Name/No

THE HIKE

Start Time

End Time

Actual Distance

Total No of Steps

Calories Burned

(M)   (P)

POINTS OF INTEREST

Difficulty Level (1 Easy 5 Hard) △

Enjoyment Level (1 Bad 5 Good) ♡

Overall Grade (1 Bad 5 Good) ☆

Notes
Facilities
Parking
Costs
Nature
Etc

MY MUNRO TOTAL

THE PLAN

Date

	MUNRO NAME	My Ref

Meet up time/ location

Area name/ Closest Town

Est. Duration

GPS / Latitude & Longitude / Grid Ref

Est. Distance

Km
Miles

Loop / Line & Back / One Way   Day Trip / Overnight/ Holiday

Local Contact

Accommodation Info

THE EQUIPMENT

A   B

Map Name/No

THE HIKE

M   P

Start Time

End Time

Actual Distance

Total No of Steps

Calories
Burned

POINTS OF INTEREST

Difficulty Level (1 Easy 5 Hard) △

Enjoyment Level (1 Bad 5 Good) ♡

Overall Grade (1 Bad 5 Good) ☆

Notes
Facilities
Parking
Costs
Nature
Etc

MY MUNRO TOTAL

THE PLAN

	MUNRO NAME	My Ref

Date

Meet up time/ location

Area name/ Closest Town

Est. Duration

GPS / Latitude & Longitude / Grid Ref

Est. Distance — Km / Miles

Loop / Line & Back / One Way   Day Trip / Overnight/ Holiday

Local Contact

Accommodation Info

THE EQUIPMENT

A   B

Map Name/No

THE HIKE

Start Time

End Time

Actual Distance

Total No of Steps

Calories Burned

M   P

POINTS OF INTEREST

Difficulty Level (1 Easy 5 Hard) △

Enjoyment Level (1 Bad 5 Good) ♡

Overall Grade (1 Bad 5 Good) ☆

Notes
Facilities
Parking
Costs
Nature
Etc

MY MUNRO TOTAL

THE PLAN

Date

MUNRO NAME

My Ref

Meet up time/ location

Area name/ Closest Town

Est. Duration

GPS / Latitude & Longitude / Grid Ref

Est. Distance

Km
Miles

Loop / Line & Back / One Way   Day Trip / Overnight/ Holiday

Local Contact

Accommodation Info

THE EQUIPMENT

A   B

Map Name/No

THE HIKE

M   P

Start Time

End Time

Actual Distance

Total No of Steps

Calories
Burned

POINTS OF INTEREST

Difficulty Level (1 Easy 5 Hard)

Enjoyment Level (1 Bad 5 Good)

Overall Grade (1 Bad 5 Good)

Notes
Facilities
Parking
Costs
Nature
Etc

MY MUNRO TOTAL

THE PLAN

Date

MUNRO NAME

My Ref

Meet up time/ location	Area name/ Closest Town
Est. Duration	GPS / Latitude & Longitude / Grid Ref
Est. Distance Km Miles	
	Loop / Line & Back / One Way Day Trip / Overnight/ Holiday
Local Contact	Accommodation Info

THE EQUIPMENT

A B

Map Name/No

THE HIKE

Start Time

End Time

Actual Distance

Total No of Steps

Calories Burned

(M)   (P)

POINTS OF INTEREST

Difficulty Level (1 Easy 5 Hard) △

Enjoyment Level (1 Bad 5 Good) ♡

Overall Grade (1 Bad 5 Good) ☆

Notes
Facilities
Parking
Costs
Nature
Etc

MY MUNRO TOTAL

THE PLAN

Date

MUNRO NAME

My Ref

Meet up time/ location

Area name/ Closest Town

Est. Duration

GPS / Latitude & Longitude / Grid Ref

Est. Distance

Km
Miles

Loop / Line & Back / One Way   Day Trip / Overnight/ Holiday

Local Contact

Accommodation Info

THE EQUIPMENT

A   B

Map Name/No

THE HIKE

Start Time

End Time

M   P

Actual Distance

Total No of Steps

POINTS OF INTEREST

Calories
Burned

Difficulty Level (1 Easy 5 Hard)

Enjoyment Level (1 Bad 5 Good)

Overall Grade (1 Bad 5 Good)

Notes
Facilities
Parking
Costs
Nature
Etc

MY MUNRO TOTAL

THE PLAN

Date

MUNRO NAME

My Ref

Meet up time/ location

Area name/ Closest Town

Est. Duration

GPS / Latitude & Longitude / Grid Ref

Est. Distance

Km
Miles

Loop / Line & Back / One Way   Day Trip / Overnight/ Holiday

Local Contact

Accommodation Info

THE EQUIPMENT

A B

Map Name/No

THE HIKE

(M) (P)

Start Time

End Time

Actual Distance

Total No of Steps

Calories
Burned

POINTS OF INTEREST

Difficulty Level (1 Easy 5 Hard) △

Enjoyment Level (1 Bad 5 Good) ♡

Overall Grade (1 Bad 5 Good) ☆

Notes
Facilities
Parking
Costs
Nature
Etc

MY MUNRO TOTAL

THE PLAN

MUNRO NAME

My Ref

Date

Meet up time/ location

Area name/ Closest Town

Est. Duration

GPS / Latitude & Longitude / Grid Ref

Est. Distance

Km
Miles

Loop / Line & Back / One Way   Day Trip / Overnight/ Holiday

Local Contact

Accommodation Info

THE EQUIPMENT

A   B

Map Name/No

THE HIKE

Start Time

End Time

M   P

Actual Distance

POINTS OF INTEREST

Total No of Steps

Calories
Burned

Difficulty Level (1 Easy 5 Hard)

Enjoyment Level (1 Bad 5 Good)

Overall Grade (1 Bad 5 Good)

Notes
Facilities
Parking
Costs
Nature
Etc

MY MUNRO TOTAL

THE PLAN

Date

MUNRO NAME

My Ref

Meet up time/ location

Area name/ Closest Town

Est. Duration

GPS / Latitude & Longitude / Grid Ref

Est. Distance

Km
Miles

Loop / Line & Back / One Way   Day Trip / Overnight/ Holiday

Local Contact

Accommodation Info

THE EQUIPMENT

A   B

Map Name/No

THE HIKE

(M) (P)

Start Time

End Time

Actual Distance

Total No of Steps

Calories
Burned

POINTS OF INTEREST

Difficulty Level (1 Easy 5 Hard) △

Enjoyment Level (1 Bad 5 Good) ♡

Overall Grade (1 Bad 5 Good) ☆

Notes
Facilities
Parking
Costs
Nature
Etc

MY MUNRO TOTAL

THE PLAN

Date

MUNRO NAME

My Ref

Meet up time/ location	Area name/ Closest Town
Est. Duration	GPS / Latitude & Longitude / Grid Ref
Est. Distance Km Miles	Loop / Line & Back / One Way Day Trip / Overnight/ Holiday
Local Contact	Accommodation Info

THE EQUIPMENT

A   B

Map Name/No

THE HIKE

M   P

Start Time

End Time

Actual Distance

Total No of Steps

Calories Burned

POINTS OF INTEREST

Difficulty Level (1 Easy 5 Hard) △

Enjoyment Level (1 Bad 5 Good) ♡

Overall Grade (1 Bad 5 Good) ☆

Notes
Facilities
Parking
Costs
Nature
Etc

MY MUNRO TOTAL

THE PLAN

Date

MUNRO NAME

My Ref

Meet up time/ location

Area name/ Closest Town

Est. Duration

GPS / Latitude & Longitude / Grid Ref

Est. Distance   Km
                       Miles

Loop / Line & Back / One Way   Day Trip / Overnight/ Holiday

Local Contact

Accommodation Info

THE EQUIPMENT

A   B

Map Name/No

THE HIKE

(M) (P)

Start Time

End Time

Actual Distance

Total No of Steps

Calories
Burned

POINTS OF INTEREST

Difficulty Level (1 Easy 5 Hard)   △

Enjoyment Level (1 Bad 5 Good)   ♡

Overall Grade (1 Bad 5 Good)   ☆

Notes
Facilities
Parking
Costs
Nature
Etc

MY MUNRO TOTAL

THE PLAN

Date

| MUNRO NAME | | My Ref |

Meet up time/ location

Area name/ Closest Town

Est. Duration

GPS / Latitude & Longitude / Grid Ref

Est. Distance

Km
Miles

Loop / Line & Back / One Way   Day Trip / Overnight/ Holiday

Local Contact

Accommodation Info

THE EQUIPMENT

A   B

Map Name/No

THE HIKE

M   P

Start Time

End Time

Actual Distance

Total No of Steps

Calories
Burned

POINTS OF INTEREST

Difficulty Level (1 Easy 5 Hard) △

Enjoyment Level (1 Bad 5 Good) ♡

Overall Grade (1 Bad 5 Good) ☆

Notes
Facilities
Parking
Costs
Nature
Etc

MY MUNRO TOTAL

THE PLAN

Date

MUNRO NAME

My Ref

Meet up time/ location

Area name/ Closest Town

Est. Duration

GPS / Latitude & Longitude / Grid Ref

Est. Distance

Km
Miles

Loop / Line & Back / One Way   Day Trip / Overnight/ Holiday

Local Contact

Accommodation Info

THE EQUIPMENT

A   B

Map Name/No

THE HIKE

Start Time

End Time

Actual Distance

Total No of Steps

Calories
Burned

POINTS OF INTEREST

Difficulty Level (1 Easy 5 Hard)

Enjoyment Level (1 Bad 5 Good)

Overall Grade (1 Bad 5 Good)

Notes
Facilities
Parking
Costs
Nature
Etc

MY MUNRO TOTAL

THE PLAN

Date

| MUNRO NAME | | My Ref |

Meet up time/ location

Area name/ Closest Town

Est. Duration

GPS / Latitude & Longitude / Grid Ref

Est. Distance

Km
Miles

Loop / Line & Back / One Way   Day Trip / Overnight/ Holiday

Local Contact

Accommodation Info

THE EQUIPMENT

A   B

Map Name/No

THE HIKE

Start Time

End Time

(M) (P)

Actual Distance

Total No of Steps

POINTS OF INTEREST

Calories
Burned

Difficulty Level (1 Easy 5 Hard) △

Enjoyment Level (1 Bad 5 Good) ♡

Overall Grade (1 Bad 5 Good) ☆

Notes
Facilities
Parking
Costs
Nature
Etc

MY MUNRO TOTAL

THE PLAN

Date

| MUNRO NAME | My Ref |

Meet up time/ location

Area name/ Closest Town

Est. Duration

GPS / Latitude & Longitude / Grid Ref

Est. Distance   Km
                   Miles

Loop / Line & Back / One Way   Day Trip / Overnight/ Holiday

Local Contact

Accommodation Info

THE EQUIPMENT

A   B

Map Name/No

THE HIKE

(M) (P)

POINTS OF INTEREST

Start Time

End Time

Actual Distance

Total No of Steps

Calories
Burned

Difficulty Level (1 Easy 5 Hard) △

Enjoyment Level (1 Bad 5 Good) ♡

Overall Grade (1 Bad 5 Good) ☆

Notes
Facilities
Parking
Costs
Nature
Etc

MY MUNRO TOTAL

THE PLAN

Date

	MUNRO NAME	My Ref

Meet up time/ location — Area name/ Closest Town

Est. Duration — GPS / Latitude & Longitude / Grid Ref

Est. Distance — Km Miles

Loop / Line & Back / One Way — Day Trip / Overnight/ Holiday

Local Contact — Accommodation Info

THE EQUIPMENT

A   B

Map Name/No

THE HIKE

Start Time

End Time

Actual Distance

Total No of Steps

Calories Burned

(M) (P)

POINTS OF INTEREST

Difficulty Level (1 Easy 5 Hard) △

Enjoyment Level (1 Bad 5 Good) ♡

Overall Grade (1 Bad 5 Good) ☆

Notes
Facilities
Parking
Costs
Nature
Etc

MY MUNRO TOTAL

THE PLAN

	MUNRO NAME	My Ref
Date		

Meet up time/ location	Area name/ Closest Town
Est. Duration	GPS / Latitude & Longitude / Grid Ref
Est. Distance Km Miles	
	Loop / Line & Back / One Way Day Trip / Overnight/ Holiday
Local Contact	Accommodation Info

THE EQUIPMENT

A   B

Map Name/No

THE HIKE

Start Time

End Time

Actual Distance

Total No of Steps   Calories
                                       Burned

(M) (P)

POINTS OF INTEREST

Difficulty Level (1 Easy 5 Hard) △

Enjoyment Level (1 Bad 5 Good) ♡

Overall Grade (1 Bad 5 Good) ☆

Notes
Facilities
Parking
Costs
Nature
Etc

MY MUNRO TOTAL

THE PLAN

MUNRO NAME

My Ref

Date

Meet up time/ location

Area name/ Closest Town

Est. Duration

GPS / Latitude & Longitude / Grid Ref

Est. Distance

Km
Miles

Loop / Line & Back / One Way   Day Trip / Overnight/ Holiday

Local Contact

Accommodation Info

THE EQUIPMENT

A   B

Map Name/No

THE HIKE

Start Time

End Time

Actual Distance

(M) (P)

Total No of Steps

Calories
Burned

POINTS OF INTEREST

Difficulty Level (1 Easy 5 Hard)

Enjoyment Level (1 Bad 5 Good)

Overall Grade (1 Bad 5 Good)

Notes
Facilities
Parking
Costs
Nature
Etc

MY MUNRO TOTAL

THE PLAN

Date

MUNRO NAME

My Ref

Meet up time/ location	Area name/ Closest Town

Est. Duration	GPS / Latitude & Longitude / Grid Ref

Est. Distance	Km / Miles

Loop / Line & Back / One Way   Day Trip / Overnight/ Holiday

Local Contact	Accommodation Info

THE EQUIPMENT

A B

Map Name/No

THE HIKE

(M) (P)

Start Time

End Time

Actual Distance

Total No of Steps

Calories Burned

POINTS OF INTEREST

Difficulty Level (1 Easy 5 Hard) △

Enjoyment Level (1 Bad 5 Good) ♡

Overall Grade (1 Bad 5 Good) ☆

Notes
Facilities
Parking
Costs
Nature
Etc

MY MUNRO TOTAL

THE PLAN

Date

	MUNRO NAME	My Ref

Meet up time/ location

Area name/ Closest Town

Est. Duration

GPS / Latitude & Longitude / Grid Ref

Est. Distance

Km
Miles

Loop / Line & Back / One Way   Day Trip / Overnight/ Holiday

Local Contact

Accommodation Info

THE EQUIPMENT

A   B

Map Name/No

THE HIKE

M   P

Start Time

End Time

Actual Distance

Total No of Steps

Calories
Burned

POINTS OF INTEREST

Difficulty Level (1 Easy 5 Hard) △

Enjoyment Level (1 Bad 5 Good) ♡

Overall Grade (1 Bad 5 Good) ☆

Notes
Facilities
Parking
Costs
Nature
Etc

MY MUNRO TOTAL

THE PLAN

Date

MUNRO NAME

My Ref

Meet up time/ location

Area name/ Closest Town

Est. Duration

GPS / Latitude & Longitude / Grid Ref

Est. Distance   Km
                       Miles

Loop / Line & Back / One Way   Day Trip / Overnight/ Holiday

Local Contact

Accommodation Info

THE EQUIPMENT

A   B

Map Name/No

THE HIKE

Start Time

End Time

M   P

Actual Distance

Total No of Steps

Calories
Burned

POINTS OF INTEREST

Difficulty Level (1 Easy 5 Hard) △

Enjoyment Level (1 Bad 5 Good) ♡

Overall Grade (1 Bad 5 Good) ☆

Notes
Facilities
Parking
Costs
Nature
Etc

MY MUNRO TOTAL

THE PLAN

Date

MUNRO NAME

My Ref

Meet up time/ location

Area name/ Closest Town

Est. Duration

GPS / Latitude & Longitude / Grid Ref

Est. Distance

Km
Miles

Loop / Line & Back / One Way   Day Trip / Overnight/ Holiday

Local Contact

Accommodation Info

THE EQUIPMENT

A   B

Map Name/No

THE HIKE

Start Time

End Time

Actual Distance

Total No of Steps

Calories
Burned

M   P

POINTS OF INTEREST

Difficulty Level (1 Easy 5 Hard) △

Enjoyment Level (1 Bad 5 Good) ♡

Overall Grade (1 Bad 5 Good) ☆

Notes
Facilities
Parking
Costs
Nature
Etc

MY MUNRO TOTAL

THE PLAN

Date

MUNRO NAME

My Ref

Meet up time/ location

Area name/ Closest Town

Est. Duration

GPS / Latitude & Longitude / Grid Ref

Est. Distance

Km
Miles

Loop / Line & Back / One Way   Day Trip / Overnight/ Holiday

Local Contact

Accommodation Info

THE EQUIPMENT

A   B

Map Name/No

THE HIKE

(M) (P)

Start Time

End Time

Actual Distance

Total No of Steps

Calories
Burned

POINTS OF INTEREST

Difficulty Level (1 Easy 5 Hard) △

Enjoyment Level (1 Bad 5 Good) ♡

Overall Grade (1 Bad 5 Good) ☆

Notes
Facilities
Parking
Costs
Nature
Etc

MY MUNRO TOTAL

THE PLAN

Date

MUNRO NAME	My Ref

Meet up time/ location

Area name/ Closest Town

Est. Duration

GPS / Latitude & Longitude / Grid Ref

Est. Distance

Km
Miles

Loop / Line & Back / One Way   Day Trip / Overnight/ Holiday

Local Contact

Accommodation Info

THE EQUIPMENT

A   B

Map Name/No

THE HIKE

(M) (P)

POINTS OF INTEREST

Start Time

End Time

Actual Distance

Total No of Steps

Calories
Burned

Difficulty Level (1 Easy 5 Hard) △

Enjoyment Level (1 Bad 5 Good) ♡

Overall Grade (1 Bad 5 Good) ☆

Notes
Facilities
Parking
Costs
Nature
Etc

MY MUNRO TOTAL

THE PLAN

MUNRO NAME

My Ref

Date

Meet up time/ location

Area name/ Closest Town

Est. Duration

GPS / Latitude & Longitude / Grid Ref

Est. Distance

Km
Miles

Loop / Line & Back / One Way   Day Trip / Overnight/ Holiday

Local Contact

Accommodation Info

THE EQUIPMENT

A   B

Map Name/No

THE HIKE

Start Time

End Time

Actual Distance

M   P

Total No of Steps

Calories
Burned

POINTS OF INTEREST

Difficulty Level (1 Easy 5 Hard) △

Enjoyment Level (1 Bad 5 Good) ♡

Overall Grade (1 Bad 5 Good) ☆

Notes
Facilities
Parking
Costs
Nature
Etc

MY MUNRO TOTAL

THE PLAN

Date

MUNRO NAME

My Ref

Meet up time/ location

Area name/ Closest Town

Est. Duration

GPS / Latitude & Longitude / Grid Ref

Est. Distance

Km
Miles

Loop / Line & Back / One Way   Day Trip / Overnight/ Holiday

Local Contact

Accommodation Info

THE EQUIPMENT

A   B

Map Name/No

THE HIKE

Start Time

End Time

Actual Distance

Total No of Steps

(M)   (P)

Calories
Burned

POINTS OF INTEREST

Difficulty Level (1 Easy 5 Hard)

Enjoyment Level (1 Bad 5 Good)

Overall Grade (1 Bad 5 Good)

Notes
Facilities
Parking
Costs
Nature
Etc

MY MUNRO TOTAL

THE PLAN

MUNRO NAME

My Ref

Date

Meet up time/ location

Area name/ Closest Town

Est. Duration

GPS / Latitude & Longitude / Grid Ref

Est. Distance

Km
Miles

Loop / Line & Back / One Way   Day Trip / Overnight/ Holiday

Local Contact

Accommodation Info

THE EQUIPMENT

A   B

Map Name/No

THE HIKE

Start Time

End Time

Actual Distance

M   P

Total No of Steps

Calories
Burned

POINTS OF INTEREST

Difficulty Level (1 Easy 5 Hard) △

Enjoyment Level (1 Bad 5 Good) ♡

Overall Grade (1 Bad 5 Good) ☆

Notes
Facilities
Parking
Costs
Nature
Etc

MY MUNRO TOTAL

THE PLAN

Date

MUNRO NAME

My Ref

Meet up time/ location

Area name/ Closest Town

Est. Duration

GPS / Latitude & Longitude / Grid Ref

Est. Distance

Km
Miles

Loop / Line & Back / One Way   Day Trip / Overnight/ Holiday

Local Contact

Accommodation Info

THE EQUIPMENT

A   B

Map Name/No

THE HIKE

M   P

Start Time

End Time

Actual Distance

Total No of Steps

Calories
Burned

POINTS OF INTEREST

Difficulty Level (1 Easy 5 Hard) △

Enjoyment Level (1 Bad 5 Good) ♡

Overall Grade (1 Bad 5 Good) ☆

Notes
Facilities
Parking
Costs
Nature
Etc

MY MUNRO TOTAL

THE PLAN

Date

MUNRO NAME

My Ref

Meet up time/ location

Area name/ Closest Town

Est. Duration

GPS / Latitude & Longitude / Grid Ref

Est. Distance

Km
Miles

Loop / Line & Back / One Way   Day Trip / Overnight/ Holiday

Local Contact

Accommodation Info

THE EQUIPMENT

A   B

Map Name/No

THE HIKE

(M) (P)

Start Time

End Time

Actual Distance

Total No of Steps

Calories
Burned

POINTS OF INTEREST

Difficulty Level (1 Easy 5 Hard) △

Enjoyment Level (1 Bad 5 Good) ♡

Overall Grade (1 Bad 5 Good) ☆

Notes
Facilities
Parking
Costs
Nature
Etc

MY MUNRO TOTAL

THE PLAN

Date

Meet up time/ location

Est. Duration

Est. Distance

Km
Miles

Local Contact

MUNRO NAME

My Ref

Area name/ Closest Town

GPS / Latitude & Longitude / Grid Ref

Loop / Line & Back / One Way   Day Trip / Overnight/ Holiday

Accommodation Info

THE EQUIPMENT

A   B

Map Name/No

THE HIKE

Start Time

End Time

Actual Distance

Total No of Steps

POINTS OF INTEREST

Calories
Burned

Difficulty Level (1 Easy 5 Hard)   △

Enjoyment Level (1 Bad 5 Good)   ♡

Overall Grade (1 Bad 5 Good)   ☆

Notes
Facilities
Parking
Costs
Nature
Etc

MY MUNRO TOTAL

THE PLAN

MUNRO NAME

My Ref

Date

| Meet up time/ location | Area name/ Closest Town |

| Est. Duration | GPS / Latitude & Longitude / Grid Ref |

| Est. Distance | Km Miles |

Loop / Line & Back / One Way   Day Trip / Overnight/ Holiday

| Local Contact | Accommodation Info |

THE EQUIPMENT

A   B

Map Name/No

THE HIKE

Start Time

End Time

Actual Distance

Total No of Steps   Calories Burned

(M)   (P)

POINTS OF INTEREST

Difficulty Level (1 Easy 5 Hard) △

Enjoyment Level (1 Bad 5 Good) ♡

Overall Grade (1 Bad 5 Good) ☆

Notes
Facilities
Parking
Costs
Nature
Etc

MY MUNRO TOTAL

THE PLAN

MUNRO NAME

My Ref

Date

Meet up time/ location

Area name/ Closest Town

Est. Duration

GPS / Latitude & Longitude / Grid Ref

Est. Distance

Km
Miles

Loop / Line & Back / One Way   Day Trip / Overnight/ Holiday

Local Contact

Accommodation Info

THE EQUIPMENT

A   B

Map Name/No

THE HIKE

Start Time

End Time

M   P

Actual Distance

Total No of Steps

POINTS OF INTEREST

Calories
Burned

Difficulty Level (1 Easy 5 Hard)

Enjoyment Level (1 Bad 5 Good)

Overall Grade (1 Bad 5 Good)

Notes
Facilities
Parking
Costs
Nature
Etc

MY MUNRO TOTAL

THE PLAN

MUNRO NAME

My Ref

Date

Meet up time/ location	Area name/ Closest Town
Est. Duration	GPS / Latitude & Longitude / Grid Ref
Est. Distance Km Miles	Loop / Line & Back / One Way Day Trip / Overnight/ Holiday
Local Contact	Accommodation Info

THE EQUIPMENT

A B

Map Name/No

THE HIKE

Start Time

End Time

(M) (P)

Actual Distance

Total No of Steps

Calories Burned

POINTS OF INTEREST

Difficulty Level (1 Easy 5 Hard) △

Enjoyment Level (1 Bad 5 Good) ♡

Overall Grade (1 Bad 5 Good) ☆

Notes
Facilities
Parking
Costs
Nature
Etc

MY MUNRO TOTAL

THE PLAN

Date

MUNRO NAME

My Ref

Meet up time/ location

Area name/ Closest Town

Est. Duration

GPS / Latitude & Longitude / Grid Ref

Est. Distance

Km
Miles

Loop / Line & Back / One Way   Day Trip / Overnight/ Holiday

Local Contact

Accommodation Info

THE EQUIPMENT

A   B

Map Name/No

THE HIKE

Start Time

End Time

Actual Distance

Total No of Steps

Calories
Burned

POINTS OF INTEREST

Difficulty Level (1 Easy 5 Hard) △

Enjoyment Level (1 Bad 5 Good) ♡

Overall Grade (1 Bad 5 Good) ☆

Notes
Facilities
Parking
Costs
Nature
Etc

MY MUNRO TOTAL

THE PLAN

MUNRO NAME

My Ref

Date

Meet up time/ location	Area name/ Closest Town

Est. Duration	GPS / Latitude & Longitude / Grid Ref

Est. Distance Km / Miles	

Loop / Line & Back / One Way   Day Trip / Overnight/ Holiday

Local Contact	Accommodation Info

THE EQUIPMENT

A   B

Map Name/No

THE HIKE

(M) (P)

Start Time

End Time

Actual Distance

Total No of Steps

Calories Burned

POINTS OF INTEREST

Difficulty Level (1 Easy 5 Hard) △

Enjoyment Level (1 Bad 5 Good) ♡

Overall Grade (1 Bad 5 Good) ☆

Notes
Facilities
Parking
Costs
Nature
Etc

MY MUNRO TOTAL

THE PLAN

Date

Meet up time/ location

Est. Duration

Est. Distance

Km
Miles

Local Contact

MUNRO NAME

My Ref

Area name/ Closest Town

GPS / Latitude & Longitude / Grid Ref

Loop / Line & Back / One Way   Day Trip / Overnight/ Holiday

Accommodation Info

THE EQUIPMENT

A   B

Map Name/No

THE HIKE

Start Time

End Time

Actual Distance

Total No of Steps

M   P

POINTS OF INTEREST

Calories
Burned

Difficulty Level (1 Easy 5 Hard)   △

Enjoyment Level (1 Bad 5 Good)   ♡

Overall Grade (1 Bad 5 Good)   ☆

Notes
Facilities
Parking
Costs
Nature
Etc

MY MUNRO TOTAL

THE PLAN

MUNRO NAME

My Ref

Date

Meet up time/ location

Area name/ Closest Town

Est. Duration

GPS / Latitude & Longitude / Grid Ref

Est. Distance

Km
Miles

Loop / Line & Back / One Way   Day Trip / Overnight/ Holiday

Local Contact

Accommodation Info

THE EQUIPMENT

A B

Map Name/No

THE HIKE

Start Time

End Time

Actual Distance

(M) (P)

Total No of Steps

Calories
Burned

POINTS OF INTEREST

Difficulty Level (1 Easy 5 Hard) △

Enjoyment Level (1 Bad 5 Good) ♡

Overall Grade (1 Bad 5 Good) ☆

Notes
Facilities
Parking
Costs
Nature
Etc

MY MUNRO TOTAL

THE PLAN

THE PLAN	**MUNRO NAME**
Date	**My Ref**

Meet up time/ location	Area name/ Closest Town
Est. Duration	GPS / Latitude & Longitude / Grid Ref
Est. Distance — Km Miles	
	Loop / Line & Back / One Way Day Trip / Overnight/ Holiday
Local Contact	Accommodation Info

THE EQUIPMENT

A   B

Map Name/No

THE HIKE

(M) (P)

Start Time

End Time

Actual Distance

Total No of Steps

POINTS OF INTEREST

Calories Burned

Difficulty Level (1 Easy 5 Hard) △

Enjoyment Level (1 Bad 5 Good) ♡

Overall Grade (1 Bad 5 Good) ☆

Notes
Facilities
Parking
Costs
Nature
Etc

MY MUNRO TOTAL

THE PLAN

Date

MUNRO NAME

My Ref

Meet up time/ location	Area name/ Closest Town
Est. Duration	GPS / Latitude & Longitude / Grid Ref
Est. Distance	Km Miles
	Loop / Line & Back / One Way Day Trip / Overnight/ Holiday
Local Contact	Accommodation Info

THE EQUIPMENT

A   B

Map Name/No

THE HIKE

M   P

Start Time

End Time

Actual Distance

Total No of Steps

Calories Burned

POINTS OF INTEREST

Difficulty Level (1 Easy 5 Hard) △

Enjoyment Level (1 Bad 5 Good) ♡

Overall Grade (1 Bad 5 Good) ☆

Notes
Facilities
Parking
Costs
Nature
Etc

MY MUNRO TOTAL

THE PLAN

Date

	MUNRO NAME	My Ref

Meet up time/ location

Area name/ Closest Town

Est. Duration

GPS / Latitude & Longitude / Grid Ref

Est. Distance Km Miles

Loop / Line & Back / One Way   Day Trip / Overnight/ Holiday

Local Contact

Accommodation Info

THE EQUIPMENT

A   B

Map Name/No

THE HIKE

(M) (P)

Start Time

End Time

Actual Distance

Total No of Steps

Calories Burned

POINTS OF INTEREST

Difficulty Level (1 Easy 5 Hard) △

Enjoyment Level (1 Bad 5 Good) ♡

Overall Grade (1 Bad 5 Good) ☆

Notes
Facilities
Parking
Costs
Nature
Etc

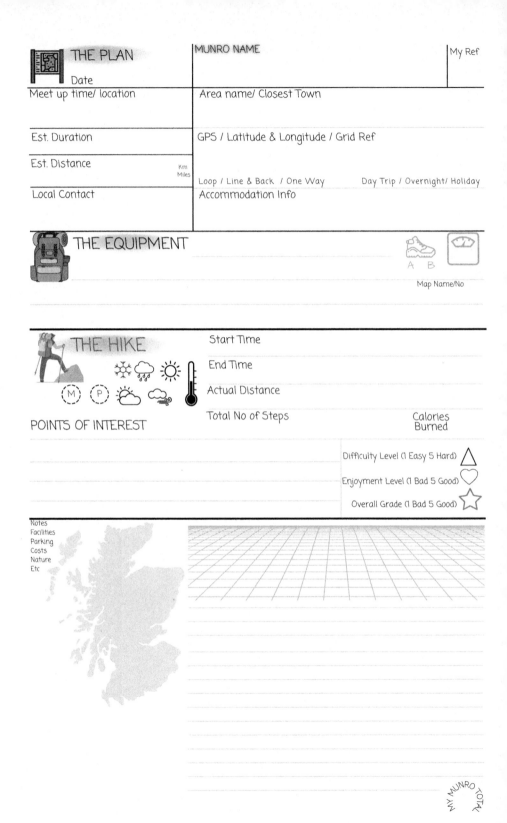

MY MUNRO TOTAL

THE PLAN

THE PLAN	**MUNRO NAME**	**My Ref**
Date		

Meet up time/ location	Area name/ Closest Town
Est. Duration	GPS / Latitude & Longitude / Grid Ref
Est. Distance Km Miles	Loop / Line & Back / One Way Day Trip / Overnight/ Holiday
Local Contact	Accommodation Info

THE EQUIPMENT

A   B

Map Name/No

THE HIKE

Start Time

End Time

Actual Distance

Total No of Steps

(M) (P)

Calories
Burned

POINTS OF INTEREST

Difficulty Level (1 Easy 5 Hard) △

Enjoyment Level (1 Bad 5 Good) ♡

Overall Grade (1 Bad 5 Good) ☆

Notes
Facilities
Parking
Costs
Nature
Etc

MY MUNRO TOTAL

THE PLAN

Date

	MUNRO NAME	My Ref

Meet up time/ location

Area name/ Closest Town

Est. Duration

GPS / Latitude & Longitude / Grid Ref

Est. Distance

Km
Miles

Loop / Line & Back / One Way   Day Trip / Overnight/ Holiday

Local Contact

Accommodation Info

THE EQUIPMENT

A   B

Map Name/No

THE HIKE

Start Time

End Time

(M) (P)

Actual Distance

Total No of Steps

Calories
Burned

POINTS OF INTEREST

Difficulty Level (1 Easy 5 Hard) △

Enjoyment Level (1 Bad 5 Good) ♡

Overall Grade (1 Bad 5 Good) ☆

Notes
Facilities
Parking
Costs
Nature
Etc

MY MUNRO TOTAL

THE PLAN

Date

MUNRO NAME

My Ref

Meet up time/ location

Area name/ Closest Town

Est. Duration

GPS / Latitude & Longitude / Grid Ref

Est. Distance

Km
Miles

Loop / Line & Back / One Way   Day Trip / Overnight/ Holiday

Local Contact

Accommodation Info

THE EQUIPMENT

A   B

Map Name/No

THE HIKE

M   P

Start Time

End Time

Actual Distance

Total No of Steps

Calories
Burned

POINTS OF INTEREST

Difficulty Level (1 Easy 5 Hard) △

Enjoyment Level (1 Bad 5 Good) ♡

Overall Grade (1 Bad 5 Good) ☆

Notes
Facilities
Parking
Costs
Nature
Etc

MY MUNRO TOTAL

THE PLAN

Date	MUNRO NAME
	My Ref

Meet up time/ location

Area name/ Closest Town

Est. Duration

GPS / Latitude & Longitude / Grid Ref

Est. Distance

Km
Miles

Loop / Line & Back / One Way   Day Trip / Overnight/ Holiday

Local Contact

Accommodation Info

THE EQUIPMENT

A B

Map Name/No

THE HIKE

Start Time

End Time

Actual Distance

Total No of Steps

M P

POINTS OF INTEREST

Calories
Burned

Difficulty Level (1 Easy 5 Hard) △

Enjoyment Level (1 Bad 5 Good) ♡

Overall Grade (1 Bad 5 Good) ☆

Notes
Facilities
Parking
Costs
Nature
Etc

MY MUNRO TOTAL

THE PLAN

Date

MUNRO NAME

My Ref

Meet up time/ location

Area name/ Closest Town

Est. Duration

GPS / Latitude & Longitude / Grid Ref

Est. Distance

Km
Miles

Loop / Line & Back / One Way   Day Trip / Overnight/ Holiday

Local Contact

Accommodation Info

THE EQUIPMENT

A   B

Map Name/No

THE HIKE

Start Time

End Time

M   P

Actual Distance

Total No of Steps

Calories
Burned

POINTS OF INTEREST

Difficulty Level (1 Easy 5 Hard) △

Enjoyment Level (1 Bad 5 Good) ♡

Overall Grade (1 Bad 5 Good) ☆

Notes
Facilities
Parking
Costs
Nature
Etc

MY MUNRO TOTAL

THE PLAN

Date

MUNRO NAME

My Ref

Meet up time/ location

Area name/ Closest Town

Est. Duration

GPS / Latitude & Longitude / Grid Ref

Est. Distance

Km
Miles

Loop / Line & Back / One Way   Day Trip / Overnight/ Holiday

Local Contact

Accommodation Info

THE EQUIPMENT

A   B

Map Name/No

THE HIKE

Start Time

End Time

Actual Distance

Total No of Steps

Calories
Burned

(M) (P)

POINTS OF INTEREST

Difficulty Level (1 Easy 5 Hard) △

Enjoyment Level (1 Bad 5 Good) ♡

Overall Grade (1 Bad 5 Good) ☆

Notes
Facilities
Parking
Costs
Nature
Etc

MY MUNRO TOTAL

THE PLAN

	MUNRO NAME	My Ref
Date		

Meet up time/ location

Area name/ Closest Town

Est. Duration

GPS / Latitude & Longitude / Grid Ref

Est. Distance   Km
                                 Miles

Loop / Line & Back / One Way   Day Trip / Overnight/ Holiday

Local Contact

Accommodation Info

THE EQUIPMENT

A   B

Map Name/No

THE HIKE

Start Time

End Time

(M)   (P)

Actual Distance

Total No of Steps   Calories
                                          Burned

POINTS OF INTEREST

Difficulty Level (1 Easy 5 Hard) △

Enjoyment Level (1 Bad 5 Good) ♡

Overall Grade (1 Bad 5 Good) ☆

Notes
Facilities
Parking
Costs
Nature
Etc

MY MUNRO TOTAL

THE PLAN

Date

	MUNRO NAME	My Ref

Meet up time/ location

Area name/ Closest Town

Est. Duration

GPS / Latitude & Longitude / Grid Ref

Est. Distance   Km
                       Miles

Loop / Line & Back / One Way   Day Trip / Overnight/ Holiday

Local Contact

Accommodation Info

THE EQUIPMENT

A   B

Map Name/No

THE HIKE

(M) (P)

Start Time

End Time

Actual Distance

POINTS OF INTEREST

Total No of Steps

Calories
Burned

Difficulty Level (1 Easy 5 Hard) △

Enjoyment Level (1 Bad 5 Good) ♡

Overall Grade (1 Bad 5 Good) ☆

Notes
Facilities
Parking
Costs
Nature
Etc

MY MUNRO TOTAL

THE PLAN

Date

MUNRO NAME

My Ref

| Meet up time/ location | Area name/ Closest Town |

| Est. Duration | GPS / Latitude & Longitude / Grid Ref |

| Est. Distance | Km Miles |

Loop / Line & Back / One Way   Day Trip / Overnight/ Holiday

| Local Contact | Accommodation Info |

THE EQUIPMENT

A B

Map Name/No

THE HIKE

(M) (P)

Start Time

End Time

Actual Distance

Total No of Steps

POINTS OF INTEREST

Calories Burned

Difficulty Level (1 Easy 5 Hard) △

Enjoyment Level (1 Bad 5 Good) ♡

Overall Grade (1 Bad 5 Good) ☆

Notes
Facilities
Parking
Costs
Nature
Etc

MY MUNRO TOTAL

THE PLAN

Date

| MUNRO NAME | My Ref |

Meet up time/ location

Area name/ Closest Town

Est. Duration

GPS / Latitude & Longitude / Grid Ref

Est. Distance

Km
Miles

Loop / Line & Back / One Way   Day Trip / Overnight/ Holiday

Local Contact

Accommodation Info

THE EQUIPMENT

A   B

Map Name/No

THE HIKE

(M) (P)

Start Time

End Time

Actual Distance

Total No of Steps

Calories
Burned

POINTS OF INTEREST

Difficulty Level (1 Easy 5 Hard) △

Enjoyment Level (1 Bad 5 Good) ♡

Overall Grade (1 Bad 5 Good) ☆

Notes
Facilities
Parking
Costs
Nature
Etc

MY MUNRO TOTAL

THE PLAN

MUNRO NAME

My Ref

Date

Meet up time/ location

Est. Duration

Est. Distance
Km
Miles

Local Contact

Area name/ Closest Town

GPS / Latitude & Longitude / Grid Ref

Loop / Line & Back / One Way   Day Trip / Overnight/ Holiday

Accommodation Info

THE EQUIPMENT

A   B

Map Name/No

THE HIKE

M   P

Start Time

End Time

Actual Distance

Total No of Steps

Calories
Burned

POINTS OF INTEREST

Difficulty Level (1 Easy 5 Hard) △

Enjoyment Level (1 Bad 5 Good) ♡

Overall Grade (1 Bad 5 Good) ☆

Notes
Facilities
Parking
Costs
Nature
Etc

MY MUNRO TOTAL

THE PLAN

Date

MUNRO NAME

My Ref

Meet up time/ location

Area name/ Closest Town

Est. Duration

GPS / Latitude & Longitude / Grid Ref

Est. Distance

Km
Miles

Loop / Line & Back / One Way   Day Trip / Overnight/ Holiday

Local Contact

Accommodation Info

THE EQUIPMENT

A   B

Map Name/No

THE HIKE

Start Time

End Time

Actual Distance

M   P

Total No of Steps

Calories
Burned

POINTS OF INTEREST

Difficulty Level (1 Easy 5 Hard) △

Enjoyment Level (1 Bad 5 Good) ♡

Overall Grade (1 Bad 5 Good) ☆

Notes
Facilities
Parking
Costs
Nature
Etc

MY MUNRO TOTAL

THE PLAN

THE PLAN	**MUNRO NAME**
Date	My Ref

Meet up time/ location

Area name/ Closest Town

Est. Duration

GPS / Latitude & Longitude / Grid Ref

Est. Distance

Km
Miles

Loop / Line & Back / One Way   Day Trip / Overnight/ Holiday

Local Contact

Accommodation Info

THE EQUIPMENT

A   B

Map Name/No

THE HIKE

(M)   (P)

Start Time

End Time

Actual Distance

Total No of Steps

Calories
Burned

POINTS OF INTEREST

Difficulty Level (1 Easy 5 Hard) △

Enjoyment Level (1 Bad 5 Good) ♡

Overall Grade (1 Bad 5 Good) ☆

Notes
Facilities
Parking
Costs
Nature
Etc

MY MUNRO TOTAL

THE PLAN
Date

MUNRO NAME

My Ref

Meet up time/ location

Area name/ Closest Town

Est. Duration

GPS / Latitude & Longitude / Grid Ref

Est. Distance

Km
Miles

Loop / Line & Back / One Way   Day Trip / Overnight/ Holiday

Local Contact

Accommodation Info

THE EQUIPMENT

A   B

Map Name/No

THE HIKE

M   P

Start Time

End Time

Actual Distance

Total No of Steps

Calories
Burned

POINTS OF INTEREST

Difficulty Level (1 Easy 5 Hard) △

Enjoyment Level (1 Bad 5 Good) ♡

Overall Grade (1 Bad 5 Good) ☆

Notes
Facilities
Parking
Costs
Nature
Etc

MY MUNRO TOTAL

THE PLAN

MUNRO NAME

My Ref

Date

Meet up time/ location	Area name/ Closest Town
Est. Duration	GPS / Latitude & Longitude / Grid Ref
Est. Distance Km Miles	Loop / Line & Back / One Way Day Trip / Overnight/ Holiday
Local Contact	Accommodation Info

THE EQUIPMENT

A   B

Map Name/No

THE HIKE

Start Time

End Time

Actual Distance

Total No of Steps

Calories Burned

(M) (P)

POINTS OF INTEREST

Difficulty Level (1 Easy 5 Hard) △

Enjoyment Level (1 Bad 5 Good) ♡

Overall Grade (1 Bad 5 Good) ☆

Notes
Facilities
Parking
Costs
Nature
Etc

MY MUNRO TOTAL

THE PLAN

Date

MUNRO NAME		My Ref

Meet up time/ location

Area name/ Closest Town

Est. Duration

GPS / Latitude & Longitude / Grid Ref

Est. Distance

Km
Miles

Loop / Line & Back / One Way   Day Trip / Overnight/ Holiday

Local Contact

Accommodation Info

THE EQUIPMENT

A   B

Map Name/No

THE HIKE

(M) (P)

Start Time

End Time

Actual Distance

Total No of Steps

POINTS OF INTEREST

Calories
Burned

Difficulty Level (1 Easy 5 Hard) △

Enjoyment Level (1 Bad 5 Good) ♡

Overall Grade (1 Bad 5 Good) ☆

Notes
Facilities
Parking
Costs
Nature
Etc

MY MUNRO TOTAL

THE PLAN

Date

MUNRO NAME

My Ref

Meet up time/ location

Area name/ Closest Town

Est. Duration

GPS / Latitude & Longitude / Grid Ref

Est. Distance

Km
Miles

Loop / Line & Back / One Way   Day Trip / Overnight/ Holiday

Local Contact

Accommodation Info

THE EQUIPMENT

A   B

Map Name/No

THE HIKE

Start Time

End Time

M   P

Actual Distance

Total No of Steps

Calories
Burned

POINTS OF INTEREST

Difficulty Level (1 Easy 5 Hard)

Enjoyment Level (1 Bad 5 Good)

Overall Grade (1 Bad 5 Good)

Notes
Facilities
Parking
Costs
Nature
Etc

MY MUNRO TOTAL

THE PLAN

Date

MUNRO NAME

My Ref

Meet up time/ location

Area name/ Closest Town

Est. Duration

GPS / Latitude & Longitude / Grid Ref

Est. Distance

Km
Miles

Loop / Line & Back / One Way   Day Trip / Overnight/ Holiday

Local Contact

Accommodation Info

THE EQUIPMENT

A   B

Map Name/No

THE HIKE

Start Time

End Time

(M)   (P)

Actual Distance

Total No of Steps

Calories
Burned

POINTS OF INTEREST

Difficulty Level (1 Easy 5 Hard)

Enjoyment Level (1 Bad 5 Good)

Overall Grade (1 Bad 5 Good)

Notes
Facilities
Parking
Costs
Nature
Etc

MY MUNRO TOTAL

THE PLAN

	MUNRO NAME	My Ref
Date		

Meet up time/ location | Area name/ Closest Town

Est. Duration | GPS / Latitude & Longitude / Grid Ref

Est. Distance — Km / Miles

Loop / Line & Back / One Way — Day Trip / Overnight/ Holiday

Local Contact | Accommodation Info

THE EQUIPMENT

A   B

Map Name/No

THE HIKE

Start Time

End Time

Actual Distance

Total No of Steps

(M)   (P)

POINTS OF INTEREST

Calories Burned

Difficulty Level (1 Easy 5 Hard) △

Enjoyment Level (1 Bad 5 Good) ♡

Overall Grade (1 Bad 5 Good) ☆

Notes
Facilities
Parking
Costs
Nature
Etc

MY MUNRO TOTAL

THE PLAN

Date

MUNRO NAME

My Ref

Meet up time/ location

Area name/ Closest Town

Est. Duration

GPS / Latitude & Longitude / Grid Ref

Est. Distance

Km
Miles

Loop / Line & Back / One Way   Day Trip / Overnight/ Holiday

Local Contact

Accommodation Info

THE EQUIPMENT

A B

Map Name/No

THE HIKE

M   P

Start Time

End Time

Actual Distance

Total No of Steps

POINTS OF INTEREST

Calories
Burned

Difficulty Level (1 Easy 5 Hard) △

Enjoyment Level (1 Bad 5 Good) ♡

Overall Grade (1 Bad 5 Good) ☆

Notes
Facilities
Parking
Costs
Nature
Etc

MY MUNRO TOTAL

THE PLAN

Date

	MUNRO NAME	My Ref

Meet up time/ location

Area name/ Closest Town

Est. Duration

GPS / Latitude & Longitude / Grid Ref

Est. Distance

Km
Miles

Loop / Line & Back / One Way   Day Trip / Overnight/ Holiday

Local Contact

Accommodation Info

THE EQUIPMENT

A   B

Map Name/No

THE HIKE

Start Time

End Time

Actual Distance

Total No of Steps

Calories
Burned

(M)   (P)

POINTS OF INTEREST

Difficulty Level (1 Easy 5 Hard) △

Enjoyment Level (1 Bad 5 Good) ♡

Overall Grade (1 Bad 5 Good) ☆

Notes
Facilities
Parking
Costs
Nature
Etc

MY MUNRO TOTAL

THE PLAN

	MUNRO NAME	My Ref

Date

Meet up time/ location	Area name/ Closest Town

Est. Duration	GPS / Latitude & Longitude / Grid Ref

Est. Distance	Km Miles	

Loop / Line & Back / One Way   Day Trip / Overnight/ Holiday

Local Contact	Accommodation Info

THE EQUIPMENT

A B

Map Name/No

THE HIKE

(M) (P)

Start Time

End Time

Actual Distance

Total No of Steps

Calories Burned

POINTS OF INTEREST

Difficulty Level (1 Easy 5 Hard) △

Enjoyment Level (1 Bad 5 Good) ♡

Overall Grade (1 Bad 5 Good) ☆

Notes
Facilities
Parking
Costs
Nature
Etc

MY MUNRO TOTAL

THE PLAN

Date

MUNRO NAME

My Ref

Meet up time/ location

Area name/ Closest Town

Est. Duration

GPS / Latitude & Longitude / Grid Ref

Est. Distance

Km
Miles

Loop / Line & Back / One Way   Day Trip / Overnight/ Holiday

Local Contact

Accommodation Info

THE EQUIPMENT

A   B

Map Name/No

THE HIKE

Start Time

End Time

Actual Distance

Total No of Steps

Calories
Burned

(M) (P)

POINTS OF INTEREST

Difficulty Level (1 Easy 5 Hard) △

Enjoyment Level (1 Bad 5 Good) ♡

Overall Grade (1 Bad 5 Good) ☆

Notes
Facilities
Parking
Costs
Nature
Etc

MY MUNRO TOTAL

THE PLAN

Date

MUNRO NAME

My Ref

Meet up time/ location

Area name/ Closest Town

Est. Duration

GPS / Latitude & Longitude / Grid Ref

Est. Distance

Km
Miles

Loop / Line & Back / One Way   Day Trip / Overnight/ Holiday

Local Contact

Accommodation Info

THE EQUIPMENT

A   B

Map Name/No

THE HIKE

Start Time

End Time

Actual Distance

M   P

Total No of Steps

Calories
Burned

POINTS OF INTEREST

Difficulty Level (1 Easy 5 Hard)

Enjoyment Level (1 Bad 5 Good)

Overall Grade (1 Bad 5 Good)

Notes
Facilities
Parking
Costs
Nature
Etc

MY MUNRO TOTAL

THE PLAN

Date

	MUNRO NAME	My Ref

Meet up time/ location

Area name/ Closest Town

Est. Duration

GPS / Latitude & Longitude / Grid Ref

Est. Distance   Km / Miles

Loop / Line & Back / One Way   Day Trip / Overnight/ Holiday

Local Contact

Accommodation Info

THE EQUIPMENT

A   B

Map Name/No

THE HIKE

(M) (P)

Start Time

End Time

Actual Distance

Total No of Steps

Calories Burned

POINTS OF INTEREST

Difficulty Level (1 Easy 5 Hard) △

Enjoyment Level (1 Bad 5 Good) ♡

Overall Grade (1 Bad 5 Good) ☆

Notes
Facilities
Parking
Costs
Nature
Etc

MY MUNRO TOTAL

THE PLAN

MUNRO NAME

My Ref

Date

Meet up time/ location

Area name/ Closest Town

Est. Duration

GPS / Latitude & Longitude / Grid Ref

Est. Distance

Km
Miles

Loop / Line & Back / One Way   Day Trip / Overnight/ Holiday

Local Contact

Accommodation Info

THE EQUIPMENT

A   B

Map Name/No

THE HIKE

Start Time

End Time

M   P

Actual Distance

Total No of Steps

Calories
Burned

POINTS OF INTEREST

Difficulty Level (1 Easy 5 Hard)

Enjoyment Level (1 Bad 5 Good)

Overall Grade (1 Bad 5 Good)

Notes
Facilities
Parking
Costs
Nature
Etc

MY MUNRO TOTAL

THE PLAN

MUNRO NAME

My Ref

Date

Meet up time/ location	Area name/ Closest Town

Est. Duration	GPS / Latitude & Longitude / Grid Ref

Est. Distance

Km
Miles

Loop / Line & Back / One Way   Day Trip / Overnight/ Holiday

Local Contact	Accommodation Info

THE EQUIPMENT

A   B

Map Name/No

THE HIKE

Start Time

End Time

(M)   (P)

Actual Distance

Total No of Steps

Calories
Burned

POINTS OF INTEREST

Difficulty Level (1 Easy 5 Hard) △

Enjoyment Level (1 Bad 5 Good) ♡

Overall Grade (1 Bad 5 Good) ☆

Notes
Facilities
Parking
Costs
Nature
Etc

MY MUNRO TOTAL

THE PLAN

Date

MUNRO NAME

My Ref

Meet up time/ location

Area name/ Closest Town

Est. Duration

GPS / Latitude & Longitude / Grid Ref

Est. Distance

Km
Miles

Loop / Line & Back / One Way   Day Trip / Overnight/ Holiday

Local Contact

Accommodation Info

THE EQUIPMENT

A   B

Map Name/No

THE HIKE

M   P

Start Time

End Time

Actual Distance

Total No of Steps

POINTS OF INTEREST

Calories
Burned

Difficulty Level (1 Easy 5 Hard) △

Enjoyment Level (1 Bad 5 Good) ♡

Overall Grade (1 Bad 5 Good) ☆

Notes
Facilities
Parking
Costs
Nature
Etc

MY MUNRO TOTAL

THE PLAN

Date

	MUNRO NAME	My Ref

Meet up time/ location

Area name/ Closest Town

Est. Duration

GPS / Latitude & Longitude / Grid Ref

Est. Distance   Km
                                 Miles

Loop / Line & Back / One Way   Day Trip / Overnight/ Holiday

Local Contact

Accommodation Info

THE EQUIPMENT

A   B

Map Name/No

THE HIKE

(M)   (P)

Start Time

End Time

Actual Distance

Total No of Steps

Calories
Burned

POINTS OF INTEREST

Difficulty Level (1 Easy 5 Hard) △

Enjoyment Level (1 Bad 5 Good) ♡

Overall Grade (1 Bad 5 Good) ☆

Notes
Facilities
Parking
Costs
Nature
Etc

MY MUNRO TOTAL

THE PLAN

Date

MUNRO NAME

My Ref

Meet up time/ location

Area name/ Closest Town

Est. Duration

GPS / Latitude & Longitude / Grid Ref

Est. Distance

Km
Miles

Loop / Line & Back / One Way   Day Trip / Overnight/ Holiday

Local Contact

Accommodation Info

THE EQUIPMENT

A   B

Map Name/No

THE HIKE

Start Time

End Time

Actual Distance

Total No of Steps

Calories
Burned

POINTS OF INTEREST

Difficulty Level (1 Easy 5 Hard) △

Enjoyment Level (1 Bad 5 Good) ♡

Overall Grade (1 Bad 5 Good) ☆

Notes
Facilities
Parking
Costs
Nature
Etc

MY MUNRO TOTAL

THE PLAN

Date

MUNRO NAME

My Ref

Meet up time/ location

Area name/ Closest Town

Est. Duration

GPS / Latitude & Longitude / Grid Ref

Est. Distance

Km
Miles

Loop / Line & Back / One Way   Day Trip / Overnight/ Holiday

Local Contact

Accommodation Info

THE EQUIPMENT

A B

Map Name/No

THE HIKE

(M) (P)

Start Time

End Time

Actual Distance

Total No of Steps

Calories Burned

POINTS OF INTEREST

Difficulty Level (1 Easy 5 Hard) △

Enjoyment Level (1 Bad 5 Good) ♡

Overall Grade (1 Bad 5 Good) ☆

Notes
Facilities
Parking
Costs
Nature
Etc

MY MUNRO TOTAL

THE PLAN

Date

MUNRO NAME	My Ref

Meet up time/ location

Area name/ Closest Town

Est. Duration

GPS / Latitude & Longitude / Grid Ref

Est. Distance   Km
                       Miles

Loop / Line & Back / One Way   Day Trip / Overnight/ Holiday

Local Contact

Accommodation Info

THE EQUIPMENT

A   B

Map Name/No

THE HIKE

Start Time

End Time

Actual Distance

Total No of Steps   Calories Burned

(M) (P)

POINTS OF INTEREST

Difficulty Level (1 Easy 5 Hard) △

Enjoyment Level (1 Bad 5 Good) ♡

Overall Grade (1 Bad 5 Good) ☆

Notes
Facilities
Parking
Costs
Nature
Etc

MY MUNRO TOTAL

THE PLAN

Date

MUNRO NAME

My Ref

Meet up time/ location

Area name/ Closest Town

Est. Duration

GPS / Latitude & Longitude / Grid Ref

Est. Distance

Km
Miles

Loop / Line & Back / One Way   Day Trip / Overnight/ Holiday

Local Contact

Accommodation Info

THE EQUIPMENT

A   B

Map Name/No

THE HIKE

(M)   (P)

Start Time

End Time

Actual Distance

Total No of Steps

Calories
Burned

POINTS OF INTEREST

Difficulty Level (1 Easy 5 Hard) △

Enjoyment Level (1 Bad 5 Good) ♡

Overall Grade (1 Bad 5 Good) ☆

Notes
Facilities
Parking
Costs
Nature
Etc

MY MUNRO TOTAL

THE PLAN

Date

MUNRO NAME

My Ref

Meet up time/ location	Area name/ Closest Town
Est. Duration	GPS / Latitude & Longitude / Grid Ref
Est. Distance — Km / Miles	Loop / Line & Back / One Way Day Trip / Overnight/ Holiday
Local Contact	Accommodation Info

THE EQUIPMENT

A   B

Map Name/No

THE HIKE

(M) (P)

Start Time

End Time

Actual Distance

Total No of Steps

Calories Burned

POINTS OF INTEREST

Difficulty Level (1 Easy 5 Hard) △

Enjoyment Level (1 Bad 5 Good) ♡

Overall Grade (1 Bad 5 Good) ☆

Notes
Facilities
Parking
Costs
Nature
Etc

MY MUNRO TOTAL

THE PLAN

Date

Meet up time/ location	
Est. Duration	
Est. Distance Km / Miles	
Local Contact	

MUNRO NAME

My Ref

Area name/ Closest Town

GPS / Latitude & Longitude / Grid Ref

Loop / Line & Back / One Way   Day Trip / Overnight/ Holiday

Accommodation Info

THE EQUIPMENT

A B

Map Name/No

THE HIKE

(M) (P)

Start Time

End Time

Actual Distance

Total No of Steps

Calories Burned

POINTS OF INTEREST

Difficulty Level (1 Easy 5 Hard) △

Enjoyment Level (1 Bad 5 Good) ♡

Overall Grade (1 Bad 5 Good) ☆

Notes
Facilities
Parking
Costs
Nature
Etc

MY MUNRO TOTAL

THE PLAN

Date

MUNRO NAME

My Ref

Meet up time/ location	Area name/ Closest Town
Est. Duration	GPS / Latitude & Longitude / Grid Ref
Est. Distance Km Miles	Loop / Line & Back / One Way Day Trip / Overnight/ Holiday
Local Contact	Accommodation Info

THE EQUIPMENT

A   B

Map Name/No

THE HIKE

(M)   (P)

Start Time

End Time

Actual Distance

Total No of Steps

Calories
Burned

POINTS OF INTEREST

Difficulty Level (1 Easy 5 Hard) △

Enjoyment Level (1 Bad 5 Good) ♡

Overall Grade (1 Bad 5 Good) ☆

Notes
Facilities
Parking
Costs
Nature
Etc

MY MUNRO TOTAL

THE PLAN

Date

MUNRO NAME

My Ref

Meet up time/ location	Area name/ Closest Town
Est. Duration	GPS / Latitude & Longitude / Grid Ref
Est. Distance Km Miles	Loop / Line & Back / One Way Day Trip / Overnight/ Holiday
Local Contact	Accommodation Info

THE EQUIPMENT

A B

Map Name/No

THE HIKE

(M) (P)

Start Time

End Time

Actual Distance

Total No of Steps

Calories Burned

POINTS OF INTEREST

Difficulty Level (1 Easy 5 Hard) △

Enjoyment Level (1 Bad 5 Good) ♡

Overall Grade (1 Bad 5 Good) ☆

Notes
Facilities
Parking
Costs
Nature
Etc

MY MUNRO TOTAL

THE PLAN

Date

MUNRO NAME		My Ref

Meet up time/ location

Area name/ Closest Town

Est. Duration

GPS / Latitude & Longitude / Grid Ref

Est. Distance

Km
Miles

Loop / Line & Back / One Way   Day Trip / Overnight/ Holiday

Local Contact

Accommodation Info

THE EQUIPMENT

A   B

Map Name/No

THE HIKE

M   P

POINTS OF INTEREST

Start Time

End Time

Actual Distance

Total No of Steps

Calories Burned

Difficulty Level (1 Easy 5 Hard) △

Enjoyment Level (1 Bad 5 Good) ♡

Overall Grade (1 Bad 5 Good) ☆

Notes
Facilities
Parking
Costs
Nature
Etc

MY MUNRO TOTAL

THE PLAN

Date

MUNRO NAME

My Ref

Meet up time/ location

Area name/ Closest Town

Est. Duration

GPS / Latitude & Longitude / Grid Ref

Est. Distance

Km
Miles

Loop / Line & Back / One Way   Day Trip / Overnight/ Holiday

Local Contact

Accommodation Info

THE EQUIPMENT

A   B

Map Name/No

THE HIKE

Start Time

End Time

Actual Distance

Total No of Steps

Calories
Burned

M   P

POINTS OF INTEREST

Difficulty Level (1 Easy 5 Hard) △

Enjoyment Level (1 Bad 5 Good) ♡

Overall Grade (1 Bad 5 Good) ☆

Notes
Facilities
Parking
Costs
Nature
Etc

MY MUNRO TOTAL

THE PLAN

Date

	MUNRO NAME	My Ref

Meet up time/ location

Area name/ Closest Town

Est. Duration

GPS / Latitude & Longitude / Grid Ref

Est. Distance

Km
Miles

Loop / Line & Back / One Way   Day Trip / Overnight/ Holiday

Local Contact

Accommodation Info

THE EQUIPMENT

A   B

Map Name/No

THE HIKE

M   P

Start Time

End Time

Actual Distance

Total No of Steps

Calories
Burned

POINTS OF INTEREST

Difficulty Level (1 Easy 5 Hard) △

Enjoyment Level (1 Bad 5 Good) ♡

Overall Grade (1 Bad 5 Good) ☆

Notes
Facilities
Parking
Costs
Nature
Etc

MY MUNRO TOTAL

THE PLAN

Date

MUNRO NAME	My Ref

Meet up time/ location

Area name/ Closest Town

Est. Duration

GPS / Latitude & Longitude / Grid Ref

Est. Distance

Km
Miles

Loop / Line & Back / One Way   Day Trip / Overnight/ Holiday

Local Contact

Accommodation Info

THE EQUIPMENT

A   B

Map Name/No

THE HIKE

M   P

Start Time

End Time

Actual Distance

Total No of Steps

Calories
Burned

POINTS OF INTEREST

Difficulty Level (1 Easy 5 Hard) △

Enjoyment Level (1 Bad 5 Good) ♡

Overall Grade (1 Bad 5 Good) ☆

Notes
Facilities
Parking
Costs
Nature
Etc

MY MUNRO TOTAL

THE PLAN

Date

MUNRO NAME	My Ref

Meet up time/ location

Area name/ Closest Town

Est. Duration

GPS / Latitude & Longitude / Grid Ref

Est. Distance

Km
Miles

Loop / Line & Back / One Way   Day Trip / Overnight/ Holiday

Local Contact

Accommodation Info

THE EQUIPMENT

A   B

Map Name/No

THE HIKE

(M) (P)

POINTS OF INTEREST

Start Time

End Time

Actual Distance

Total No of Steps

Calories
Burned

Difficulty Level (1 Easy 5 Hard) △

Enjoyment Level (1 Bad 5 Good) ♡

Overall Grade (1 Bad 5 Good) ☆

Notes
Facilities
Parking
Costs
Nature
Etc

MY MUNRO TOTAL

THE PLAN

	MUNRO NAME	My Ref
Date		

Meet up time/ location | Area name/ Closest Town

Est. Duration | GPS / Latitude & Longitude / Grid Ref

Est. Distance   Km
                       Miles

Loop / Line & Back / One Way   Day Trip / Overnight/ Holiday

Local Contact | Accommodation Info

THE EQUIPMENT

A B

Map Name/No

THE HIKE

(M) (P)

Start Time

End Time

Actual Distance

Total No of Steps   Calories
                           Burned

POINTS OF INTEREST

Difficulty Level (1 Easy 5 Hard) △

Enjoyment Level (1 Bad 5 Good) ♡

Overall Grade (1 Bad 5 Good) ☆

Notes
Facilities
Parking
Costs
Nature
Etc

MY MUNRO TOTAL

THE PLAN

Date

MUNRO NAME	My Ref

Meet up time/ location

Area name/ Closest Town

Est. Duration

GPS / Latitude & Longitude / Grid Ref

Est. Distance   Km
                        Miles

Loop / Line & Back / One Way   Day Trip / Overnight/ Holiday

Local Contact

Accommodation Info

THE EQUIPMENT

A   B

Map Name/No

THE HIKE

Start Time

End Time

Actual Distance

Total No of Steps

(M)   (P)

POINTS OF INTEREST

Calories
Burned

Difficulty Level (1 Easy 5 Hard)   △

Enjoyment Level (1 Bad 5 Good)   ♡

Overall Grade (1 Bad 5 Good)   ☆

Notes
Facilities
Parking
Costs
Nature
Etc

MY MUNRO TOTAL

THE PLAN

Date

MUNRO NAME

My Ref

Meet up time/ location

Area name/ Closest Town

Est. Duration

GPS / Latitude & Longitude / Grid Ref

Est. Distance

Km
Miles

Loop / Line & Back / One Way   Day Trip / Overnight/ Holiday

Local Contact

Accommodation Info

THE EQUIPMENT

A   B

Map Name/No

THE HIKE

M   P

Start Time

End Time

Actual Distance

Total No of Steps

Calories
Burned

POINTS OF INTEREST

Difficulty Level (1 Easy 5 Hard) △

Enjoyment Level (1 Bad 5 Good) ♡

Overall Grade (1 Bad 5 Good) ☆

Notes
Facilities
Parking
Costs
Nature
Etc

MY MUNRO TOTAL

THE PLAN

Date

MUNRO NAME

My Ref

Meet up time/ location

Area name/ Closest Town

Est. Duration

GPS / Latitude & Longitude / Grid Ref

Est. Distance

Km
Miles

Loop / Line & Back / One Way   Day Trip / Overnight/ Holiday

Local Contact

Accommodation Info

THE EQUIPMENT

A   B

Map Name/No

THE HIKE

(M) (P)

Start Time

End Time

Actual Distance

Total No of Steps

Calories
Burned

POINTS OF INTEREST

Difficulty Level (1 Easy 5 Hard) △

Enjoyment Level (1 Bad 5 Good) ♡

Overall Grade (1 Bad 5 Good) ☆

Notes
Facilities
Parking
Costs
Nature
Etc

MY MUNRO TOTAL

THE PLAN

Date

Meet up time/ location

Est. Duration

Est. Distance   Km
                                 Miles

Local Contact

MUNRO NAME   My Ref

Area name/ Closest Town

GPS / Latitude & Longitude / Grid Ref

Loop / Line & Back / One Way   Day Trip / Overnight/ Holiday

Accommodation Info

THE EQUIPMENT

A B

Map Name/No

THE HIKE

Start Time

End Time

Actual Distance

Total No of Steps

M   P

POINTS OF INTEREST

Calories
Burned

Difficulty Level (1 Easy 5 Hard) △

Enjoyment Level (1 Bad 5 Good) ♡

Overall Grade (1 Bad 5 Good) ☆

Notes
Facilities
Parking
Costs
Nature
Etc

MY MUNRO TOTAL

THE PLAN

Date

MUNRO NAME

My Ref

Meet up time/ location

Area name/ Closest Town

Est. Duration

GPS / Latitude & Longitude / Grid Ref

Est. Distance
Km
Miles

Loop / Line & Back / One Way   Day Trip / Overnight/ Holiday

Local Contact

Accommodation Info

THE EQUIPMENT

A   B

Map Name/No

THE HIKE

M   P

Start Time

End Time

Actual Distance

Total No of Steps

Calories Burned

POINTS OF INTEREST

Difficulty Level (1 Easy 5 Hard) △

Enjoyment Level (1 Bad 5 Good) ♡

Overall Grade (1 Bad 5 Good) ☆

Notes
Facilities
Parking
Costs
Nature
Etc

MY MUNRO TOTAL

THE PLAN

Date

MUNRO NAME

My Ref

Meet up time/ location	Area name/ Closest Town
Est. Duration	GPS / Latitude & Longitude / Grid Ref
Est. Distance Km / Miles	Loop / Line & Back / One Way Day Trip / Overnight/ Holiday
Local Contact	Accommodation Info

THE EQUIPMENT

A   B

Map Name/No

THE HIKE

Start Time

End Time

Actual Distance

Total No of Steps

M   P

Calories
Burned

POINTS OF INTEREST

Difficulty Level (1 Easy 5 Hard) △

Enjoyment Level (1 Bad 5 Good) ♡

Overall Grade (1 Bad 5 Good) ☆

Notes
Facilities
Parking
Costs
Nature
Etc

MY MUNRO TOTAL

THE PLAN

Date

MUNRO NAME

My Ref

Meet up time/ location

Area name/ Closest Town

Est. Duration

GPS / Latitude & Longitude / Grid Ref

Est. Distance

Km
Miles

Loop / Line & Back / One Way   Day Trip / Overnight/ Holiday

Local Contact

Accommodation Info

THE EQUIPMENT

A   B

Map Name/No

THE HIKE

Start Time

End Time

Actual Distance

Total No of Steps

(M) (P)

Calories
Burned

POINTS OF INTEREST

Difficulty Level (1 Easy 5 Hard)

Enjoyment Level (1 Bad 5 Good)

Overall Grade (1 Bad 5 Good)

Notes
Facilities
Parking
Costs
Nature
Etc

MY MUNRO TOTAL

THE PLAN

Date

MUNRO NAME

My Ref

Meet up time/ location

Area name/ Closest Town

Est. Duration

GPS / Latitude & Longitude / Grid Ref

Est. Distance

Km
Miles

Loop / Line & Back / One Way   Day Trip / Overnight/ Holiday

Local Contact

Accommodation Info

THE EQUIPMENT

A   B

Map Name/No

THE HIKE

Start Time

End Time

Actual Distance

Total No of Steps

Calories
Burned

POINTS OF INTEREST

Difficulty Level (1 Easy 5 Hard) △

Enjoyment Level (1 Bad 5 Good) ♡

Overall Grade (1 Bad 5 Good) ☆

Notes
Facilities
Parking
Costs
Nature
Etc

MY MUNRO TOTAL

THE PLAN

MUNRO NAME

My Ref

Date

Meet up time/ location

Area name/ Closest Town

Est. Duration

GPS / Latitude & Longitude / Grid Ref

Est. Distance

Km
Miles

Loop / Line & Back / One Way   Day Trip / Overnight/ Holiday

Local Contact

Accommodation Info

THE EQUIPMENT

A   B

Map Name/No

THE HIKE

Start Time

End Time

Actual Distance

POINTS OF INTEREST

Total No of Steps

Calories
Burned

Difficulty Level (1 Easy 5 Hard)

Enjoyment Level (1 Bad 5 Good)

Overall Grade (1 Bad 5 Good)

Notes
Facilities
Parking
Costs
Nature
Etc

MY MUNRO TOTAL

THE PLAN

Date

MUNRO NAME		My Ref

Meet up time/ location

Area name/ Closest Town

Est. Duration

GPS / Latitude & Longitude / Grid Ref

Est. Distance

Km
Miles

Loop / Line & Back / One Way   Day Trip / Overnight/ Holiday

Local Contact

Accommodation Info

THE EQUIPMENT

A B

Map Name/No

THE HIKE

M   P

Start Time

End Time

Actual Distance

Total No of Steps

Calories
Burned

POINTS OF INTEREST

Difficulty Level (1 Easy 5 Hard) △

Enjoyment Level (1 Bad 5 Good) ♡

Overall Grade (1 Bad 5 Good) ☆

Notes
Facilities
Parking
Costs
Nature
Etc

MY MUNRO TOTAL

THE PLAN

Date

Meet up time/ location

Est. Duration

Est. Distance _____ Km
Miles

Local Contact

MUNRO NAME

My Ref

Area name/ Closest Town

GPS / Latitude & Longitude / Grid Ref

Loop / Line & Back / One Way   Day Trip / Overnight/ Holiday

Accommodation Info

THE EQUIPMENT

A   B

Map Name/No

THE HIKE

M   P

Start Time

End Time

Actual Distance

Total No of Steps

Calories
Burned

POINTS OF INTEREST

Difficulty Level (1 Easy 5 Hard) △

Enjoyment Level (1 Bad 5 Good) ♡

Overall Grade (1 Bad 5 Good) ☆

Notes
Facilities
Parking
Costs
Nature
Etc

MY MUNRO TOTAL

THE PLAN

Date

MUNRO NAME

My Ref

| Meet up time/ location | Area name/ Closest Town |

| Est. Duration | GPS / Latitude & Longitude / Grid Ref |

| Est. Distance   Km Miles | |

Loop / Line & Back / One Way   Day Trip / Overnight/ Holiday

| Local Contact | Accommodation Info |

THE EQUIPMENT

A B

Map Name/No

THE HIKE

(M) (P)

Start Time

End Time

Actual Distance

Total No of Steps

Calories Burned

POINTS OF INTEREST

Difficulty Level (1 Easy 5 Hard) △

Enjoyment Level (1 Bad 5 Good) ♡

Overall Grade (1 Bad 5 Good) ☆

Notes
Facilities
Parking
Costs
Nature
Etc

MY MUNRO TOTAL

THE PLAN

Date

	MUNRO NAME	My Ref

Meet up time/ location

Area name/ Closest Town

Est. Duration

GPS / Latitude & Longitude / Grid Ref

Est. Distance

Km
Miles

Loop / Line & Back / One Way   Day Trip / Overnight/ Holiday

Local Contact

Accommodation Info

THE EQUIPMENT

A   B

Map Name/No

THE HIKE

(M)   (P)

POINTS OF INTEREST

Start Time

End Time

Actual Distance

Total No of Steps

Calories
Burned

Difficulty Level (1 Easy 5 Hard) △

Enjoyment Level (1 Bad 5 Good) ♡

Overall Grade (1 Bad 5 Good) ☆

Notes
Facilities
Parking
Costs
Nature
Etc

MY MUNRO TOTAL

THE PLAN

Date

MUNRO NAME	My Ref

Meet up time/ location

Area name/ Closest Town

Est. Duration

GPS / Latitude & Longitude / Grid Ref

Est. Distance

Km
Miles

Loop / Line & Back / One Way   Day Trip / Overnight/ Holiday

Local Contact

Accommodation Info

THE EQUIPMENT

A   B

Map Name/No

THE HIKE

(M) (P)

Start Time

End Time

Actual Distance

Total No of Steps

Calories
Burned

POINTS OF INTEREST

Difficulty Level (1 Easy 5 Hard) △

Enjoyment Level (1 Bad 5 Good) ♡

Overall Grade (1 Bad 5 Good) ☆

Notes
Facilities
Parking
Costs
Nature
Etc

MY MUNRO TOTAL

THE PLAN

Date

MUNRO NAME		**My Ref**

Meet up time/ location

Area name/ Closest Town

Est. Duration

GPS / Latitude & Longitude / Grid Ref

Est. Distance

Km
Miles

Loop / Line & Back / One Way   Day Trip / Overnight/ Holiday

Local Contact

Accommodation Info

THE EQUIPMENT

A   B

Map Name/No

THE HIKE

(M) (P)

Start Time

End Time

Actual Distance

Total No of Steps

Calories Burned

POINTS OF INTEREST

Difficulty Level (1 Easy 5 Hard) △

Enjoyment Level (1 Bad 5 Good) ♡

Overall Grade (1 Bad 5 Good) ☆

Notes
Facilities
Parking
Costs
Nature
Etc

MY MUNRO TOTAL

THE PLAN

MUNRO NAME

My Ref

Date

Meet up time/ location

Area name/ Closest Town

Est. Duration

GPS / Latitude & Longitude / Grid Ref

Est. Distance

Km
Miles

Loop / Line & Back / One Way   Day Trip / Overnight/ Holiday

Local Contact

Accommodation Info

THE EQUIPMENT

A   B

Map Name/No

THE HIKE

Start Time

End Time

M   P

Actual Distance

Total No of Steps

Calories
Burned

POINTS OF INTEREST

Difficulty Level (1 Easy 5 Hard)

Enjoyment Level (1 Bad 5 Good)

Overall Grade (1 Bad 5 Good)

Notes
Facilities
Parking
Costs
Nature
Etc

MY MUNRO TOTAL

THE PLAN

Date

Meet up time/ location

Est. Duration

Est. Distance
Km
Miles

Local Contact

MUNRO NAME

My Ref

Area name/ Closest Town

GPS / Latitude & Longitude / Grid Ref

Loop / Line & Back / One Way   Day Trip / Overnight/ Holiday

Accommodation Info

THE EQUIPMENT

A B

Map Name/No

THE HIKE

M   P

Start Time

End Time

Actual Distance

Total No of Steps

Calories
Burned

POINTS OF INTEREST

Difficulty Level (1 Easy 5 Hard) △

Enjoyment Level (1 Bad 5 Good) ♡

Overall Grade (1 Bad 5 Good) ☆

Notes
Facilities
Parking
Costs
Nature
Etc

MY MUNRO TOTAL

THE PLAN

	MUNRO NAME	My Ref
Date		

Meet up time/ location	Area name/ Closest Town
Est. Duration	GPS / Latitude & Longitude / Grid Ref
Est. Distance Km Miles	Loop / Line & Back / One Way Day Trip / Overnight/ Holiday
Local Contact	Accommodation Info

THE EQUIPMENT

A   B

Map Name/No

THE HIKE

(M) (P)

Start Time

End Time

Actual Distance

Total No of Steps

Calories Burned

POINTS OF INTEREST

Difficulty Level (1 Easy 5 Hard) △

Enjoyment Level (1 Bad 5 Good) ♡

Overall Grade (1 Bad 5 Good) ☆

Notes
Facilities
Parking
Costs
Nature
Etc

MY MUNRO TOTAL

THE PLAN

Date

MUNRO NAME

My Ref

Meet up time/ location

Area name/ Closest Town

Est. Duration

GPS / Latitude & Longitude / Grid Ref

Est. Distance

Km
Miles

Loop / Line & Back / One Way   Day Trip / Overnight/ Holiday

Local Contact

Accommodation Info

THE EQUIPMENT

A   B

Map Name/No

THE HIKE

Start Time

End Time

Actual Distance

M   P

Total No of Steps

POINTS OF INTEREST

Calories
Burned

Difficulty Level (1 Easy 5 Hard) △

Enjoyment Level (1 Bad 5 Good) ♡

Overall Grade (1 Bad 5 Good) ☆

Notes
Facilities
Parking
Costs
Nature
Etc

MY MUNRO TOTAL

THE PLAN

Date

MUNRO NAME

My Ref

Meet up time/ location

Area name/ Closest Town

Est. Duration

GPS / Latitude & Longitude / Grid Ref

Est. Distance

Km
Miles

Loop / Line & Back / One Way   Day Trip / Overnight/ Holiday

Local Contact

Accommodation Info

THE EQUIPMENT

A   B

Map Name/No

THE HIKE

Start Time

End Time

Actual Distance

(M)   (P)

Total No of Steps

Calories
Burned

POINTS OF INTEREST

Difficulty Level (1 Easy 5 Hard) △

Enjoyment Level (1 Bad 5 Good) ♡

Overall Grade (1 Bad 5 Good) ☆

Notes
Facilities
Parking
Costs
Nature
Etc

MY MUNRO TOTAL

THE PLAN

Date

MUNRO NAME

My Ref

Meet up time/ location

Area name/ Closest Town

Est. Duration

GPS / Latitude & Longitude / Grid Ref

Est. Distance

Km
Miles

Loop / Line & Back / One Way   Day Trip / Overnight/ Holiday

Local Contact

Accommodation Info

THE EQUIPMENT

A   B

Map Name/No

THE HIKE

Start Time

End Time

Actual Distance

Total No of Steps

Calories
Burned

POINTS OF INTEREST

Difficulty Level (1 Easy 5 Hard)

Enjoyment Level (1 Bad 5 Good)

Overall Grade (1 Bad 5 Good)

Notes
Facilities
Parking
Costs
Nature
Etc

MY MUNRO TOTAL

THE PLAN

MUNRO NAME

My Ref

Date

Meet up time/ location

Area name/ Closest Town

Est. Duration

GPS / Latitude & Longitude / Grid Ref

Est. Distance

Km
Miles

Loop / Line & Back / One Way   Day Trip / Overnight/ Holiday

Local Contact

Accommodation Info

THE EQUIPMENT

A   B

Map Name/No

THE HIKE

Start Time

End Time

Actual Distance

Total No of Steps

(M)   (P)

POINTS OF INTEREST

Calories
Burned

Difficulty Level (1 Easy 5 Hard)

Enjoyment Level (1 Bad 5 Good)

Overall Grade (1 Bad 5 Good)

Notes
Facilities
Parking
Costs
Nature
Etc

MY MUNRO TOTAL

THE PLAN

Date

	MUNRO NAME	My Ref

Meet up time/ location

Area name/ Closest Town

Est. Duration

GPS / Latitude & Longitude / Grid Ref

Est. Distance

Km
Miles

Loop / Line & Back / One Way   Day Trip / Overnight/ Holiday

Local Contact

Accommodation Info

THE EQUIPMENT

A   B

Map Name/No

THE HIKE

M   P

Start Time

End Time

Actual Distance

Total No of Steps

Calories
Burned

POINTS OF INTEREST

Difficulty Level (1 Easy 5 Hard)

Enjoyment Level (1 Bad 5 Good)

Overall Grade (1 Bad 5 Good)

Notes
Facilities
Parking
Costs
Nature
Etc

MY MUNRO TOTAL

THE PLAN

	MUNRO NAME	My Ref

Date

Meet up time/ location	Area name/ Closest Town

Est. Duration	GPS / Latitude & Longitude / Grid Ref

Est. Distance Km Miles	

Loop / Line & Back / One Way   Day Trip / Overnight/ Holiday

Local Contact	Accommodation Info

THE EQUIPMENT

A   B

Map Name/No

THE HIKE

M   P

POINTS OF INTEREST

Start Time

End Time

Actual Distance

Total No of Steps

Calories Burned

Difficulty Level (1 Easy 5 Hard) △

Enjoyment Level (1 Bad 5 Good) ♡

Overall Grade (1 Bad 5 Good) ☆

Notes
Facilities
Parking
Costs
Nature
Etc

MY MUNRO TOTAL

THE PLAN

Date

MUNRO NAME

My Ref

Meet up time/ location

Area name/ Closest Town

Est. Duration

GPS / Latitude & Longitude / Grid Ref

Est. Distance

Km
Miles

Loop / Line & Back / One Way

Day Trip / Overnight/ Holiday

Local Contact

Accommodation Info

THE EQUIPMENT

A   B

Map Name/No

THE HIKE

(M) (P)

Start Time

End Time

Actual Distance

Total No of Steps

Calories
Burned

POINTS OF INTEREST

Difficulty Level (1 Easy 5 Hard) △

Enjoyment Level (1 Bad 5 Good) ♡

Overall Grade (1 Bad 5 Good) ☆

Notes
Facilities
Parking
Costs
Nature
Etc

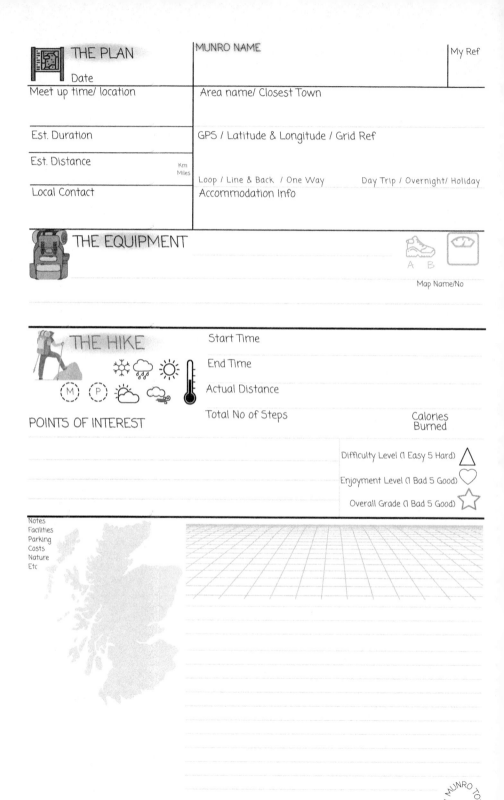

MY MUNRO TOTAL

THE PLAN

Date

MUNRO NAME

My Ref

Meet up time/ location

Area name/ Closest Town

Est. Duration

GPS / Latitude & Longitude / Grid Ref

Est. Distance

Km
Miles

Loop / Line & Back / One Way   Day Trip / Overnight/ Holiday

Local Contact

Accommodation Info

THE EQUIPMENT

A   B

Map Name/No

THE HIKE

Start Time

End Time

Actual Distance

M   P

Total No of Steps

Calories
Burned

POINTS OF INTEREST

Difficulty Level (1 Easy 5 Hard)

Enjoyment Level (1 Bad 5 Good)

Overall Grade (1 Bad 5 Good)

Notes
Facilities
Parking
Costs
Nature
Etc

MY MUNRO TOTAL

THE PLAN

MUNRO NAME

My Ref

Date

Meet up time/ location

Area name/ Closest Town

Est. Duration

GPS / Latitude & Longitude / Grid Ref

Est. Distance

Km
Miles

Loop / Line & Back / One Way   Day Trip / Overnight/ Holiday

Local Contact

Accommodation Info

THE EQUIPMENT

A   B

Map Name/No

THE HIKE

Start Time

End Time

Actual Distance

Total No of Steps

Calories
Burned

POINTS OF INTEREST

Difficulty Level (1 Easy 5 Hard) △

Enjoyment Level (1 Bad 5 Good) ♡

Overall Grade (1 Bad 5 Good) ☆

Notes
Facilities
Parking
Costs
Nature
Etc

MY MUNRO TOTAL

THE PLAN

Date

MUNRO NAME

My Ref

Meet up time/ location

Area name/ Closest Town

Est. Duration

GPS / Latitude & Longitude / Grid Ref

Est. Distance

Km
Miles

Loop / Line & Back / One Way   Day Trip / Overnight/ Holiday

Local Contact

Accommodation Info

THE EQUIPMENT

A   B

Map Name/No

THE HIKE

Start Time

End Time

Actual Distance

Total No of Steps

Calories
Burned

(M)   (P)

POINTS OF INTEREST

Difficulty Level (1 Easy 5 Hard) △

Enjoyment Level (1 Bad 5 Good) ♡

Overall Grade (1 Bad 5 Good) ☆

Notes
Facilities
Parking
Costs
Nature
Etc

MY MUNRO TOTAL

THE PLAN

MUNRO NAME

My Ref

Date

Meet up time/ location	Area name/ Closest Town
Est. Duration	GPS / Latitude & Longitude / Grid Ref
Est. Distance Km Miles	Loop / Line & Back / One Way Day Trip / Overnight/ Holiday
Local Contact	Accommodation Info

THE EQUIPMENT

A   B

Map Name/No

THE HIKE

Start Time

End Time

Actual Distance

Total No of Steps

Calories Burned

POINTS OF INTEREST

Difficulty Level (1 Easy 5 Hard) △

Enjoyment Level (1 Bad 5 Good) ♡

Overall Grade (1 Bad 5 Good) ☆

Notes
Facilities
Parking
Costs
Nature
Etc

MY MUNRO TOTAL

THE PLAN

Date

MUNRO NAME

My Ref

Meet up time/ location	Area name/ Closest Town

Est. Duration	GPS / Latitude & Longitude / Grid Ref

Est. Distance

Km
Miles

Loop / Line & Back / One Way   Day Trip / Overnight/ Holiday

Local Contact	Accommodation Info

THE EQUIPMENT

A   B

Map Name/No

THE HIKE

(M)   (P)

Start Time

End Time

Actual Distance

Total No of Steps

Calories
Burned

POINTS OF INTEREST

Difficulty Level (1 Easy 5 Hard) △

Enjoyment Level (1 Bad 5 Good) ♡

Overall Grade (1 Bad 5 Good) ☆

Notes
Facilities
Parking
Costs
Nature
Etc

MY MUNRO TOTAL

THE PLAN

Date

MUNRO NAME

My Ref

| Meet up time/ location | Area name/ Closest Town |

| Est. Duration | GPS / Latitude & Longitude / Grid Ref |

| Est. Distance | Km Miles |

Loop / Line & Back / One Way   Day Trip / Overnight/ Holiday

| Local Contact | Accommodation Info |

THE EQUIPMENT

A   B

Map Name/No

THE HIKE

(M) (P)

Start Time

End Time

Actual Distance

Total No of Steps

POINTS OF INTEREST

Calories Burned

Difficulty Level (1 Easy 5 Hard) △

Enjoyment Level (1 Bad 5 Good) ♡

Overall Grade (1 Bad 5 Good) ☆

Notes
Facilities
Parking
Costs
Nature
Etc

MY MUNRO TOTAL

THE PLAN

	MUNRO NAME	My Ref
Date		

Meet up time/ location	Area name/ Closest Town

Est. Duration	GPS / Latitude & Longitude / Grid Ref

Est. Distance	Km Miles	

Loop / Line & Back / One Way   Day Trip / Overnight/ Holiday

Local Contact	Accommodation Info

THE EQUIPMENT

A   B

Map Name/No

THE HIKE

(M) (P)

Start Time
End Time
Actual Distance
Total No of Steps	Calories Burned

POINTS OF INTEREST

Difficulty Level (1 Easy 5 Hard) △

Enjoyment Level (1 Bad 5 Good) ♡

Overall Grade (1 Bad 5 Good) ☆

Notes
Facilities
Parking
Costs
Nature
Etc

MY MUNRO TOTAL

THE PLAN

	MUNRO NAME	My Ref

Date

Meet up time/ location	Area name/ Closest Town

Est. Duration	GPS / Latitude & Longitude / Grid Ref

Est. Distance	Km Miles	

Loop / Line & Back / One Way   Day Trip / Overnight/ Holiday

Local Contact	Accommodation Info

THE EQUIPMENT

A   B

Map Name/No

THE HIKE

Start Time

End Time

Actual Distance

Total No of Steps

M   P

Calories
Burned

POINTS OF INTEREST

Difficulty Level (1 Easy 5 Hard) △

Enjoyment Level (1 Bad 5 Good) ♡

Overall Grade (1 Bad 5 Good) ☆

Notes
Facilities
Parking
Costs
Nature
Etc

MY MUNRO TOTAL

THE PLAN

Date

MUNRO NAME	My Ref

Meet up time/ location

Area name/ Closest Town

Est. Duration

GPS / Latitude & Longitude / Grid Ref

Est. Distance
Km
Miles

Loop / Line & Back / One Way   Day Trip / Overnight/ Holiday

Local Contact

Accommodation Info

THE EQUIPMENT

A   B

Map Name/No

THE HIKE

(M)   (P)

Start Time

End Time

Actual Distance

Total No of Steps

Calories
Burned

POINTS OF INTEREST

Difficulty Level (1 Easy 5 Hard) △

Enjoyment Level (1 Bad 5 Good) ♡

Overall Grade (1 Bad 5 Good) ☆

Notes
Facilities
Parking
Costs
Nature
Etc

MY MUNRO TOTAL

THE PLAN

MUNRO NAME

My Ref

Date

Meet up time/ location

Area name/ Closest Town

Est. Duration

GPS / Latitude & Longitude / Grid Ref

Est. Distance

Km
Miles

Loop / Line & Back / One Way   Day Trip / Overnight/ Holiday

Local Contact

Accommodation Info

THE EQUIPMENT

A   B

Map Name/No

THE HIKE

Start Time

End Time

Actual Distance

M   P

Total No of Steps

Calories
Burned

POINTS OF INTEREST

Difficulty Level (1 Easy 5 Hard) △

Enjoyment Level (1 Bad 5 Good) ♡

Overall Grade (1 Bad 5 Good) ☆

Notes
Facilities
Parking
Costs
Nature
Etc

MY MUNRO TOTAL

THE PLAN

MUNRO NAME

My Ref

Date

Meet up time/ location

Area name/ Closest Town

Est. Duration

GPS / Latitude & Longitude / Grid Ref

Est. Distance

Km
Miles

Loop / Line & Back / One Way   Day Trip / Overnight/ Holiday

Local Contact

Accommodation Info

THE EQUIPMENT

A B

Map Name/No

THE HIKE

(M) (P)

Start Time

End Time

Actual Distance

Total No of Steps

Calories
Burned

POINTS OF INTEREST

Difficulty Level (1 Easy 5 Hard) △

Enjoyment Level (1 Bad 5 Good) ♡

Overall Grade (1 Bad 5 Good) ☆

Notes
Facilities
Parking
Costs
Nature
Etc

MY MUNRO TOTAL

THE PLAN

	MUNRO NAME	My Ref

Date

Meet up time/ location	Area name/ Closest Town

Est. Duration	GPS / Latitude & Longitude / Grid Ref

Est. Distance Km Miles	

Loop / Line & Back / One Way   Day Trip / Overnight/ Holiday

Local Contact	Accommodation Info

THE EQUIPMENT

A   B

Map Name/No

THE HIKE

Start Time

End Time

M   P

Actual Distance

Total No of Steps

POINTS OF INTEREST

Calories
Burned

Difficulty Level (1 Easy 5 Hard) △

Enjoyment Level (1 Bad 5 Good) ♡

Overall Grade (1 Bad 5 Good) ☆

Notes
Facilities
Parking
Costs
Nature
Etc

MY MUNRO TOTAL

THE PLAN

Date

| MUNRO NAME | My Ref |

Meet up time/ location

Area name/ Closest Town

Est. Duration

GPS / Latitude & Longitude / Grid Ref

Est. Distance

Km
Miles

Loop / Line & Back / One Way   Day Trip / Overnight/ Holiday

Local Contact

Accommodation Info

THE EQUIPMENT

A   B

Map Name/No

THE HIKE

Start Time

End Time

Actual Distance

Total No of Steps

Calories
Burned

POINTS OF INTEREST

Difficulty Level (1 Easy 5 Hard) △

Enjoyment Level (1 Bad 5 Good) ♡

Overall Grade (1 Bad 5 Good) ☆

Notes
Facilities
Parking
Costs
Nature
Etc

MY MUNRO TOTAL

THE PLAN

	MUNRO NAME	My Ref
Date		

Meet up time/ location

Area name/ Closest Town

Est. Duration

GPS / Latitude & Longitude / Grid Ref

Est. Distance

Km
Miles

Loop / Line & Back / One Way   Day Trip / Overnight/ Holiday

Local Contact

Accommodation Info

THE EQUIPMENT

A   B

Map Name/No

THE HIKE

(M) (P)

Start Time

End Time

Actual Distance

Total No of Steps

Calories
Burned

POINTS OF INTEREST

Difficulty Level (1 Easy 5 Hard) △

Enjoyment Level (1 Bad 5 Good) ♡

Overall Grade (1 Bad 5 Good) ☆

Notes
Facilities
Parking
Costs
Nature
Etc

MY MUNRO TOTAL

THE PLAN

Date

| MUNRO NAME | My Ref |

Meet up time/ location

Area name/ Closest Town

Est. Duration

GPS / Latitude & Longitude / Grid Ref

Est. Distance   Km
                       Miles

Loop / Line & Back / One Way   Day Trip / Overnight/ Holiday

Local Contact

Accommodation Info

THE EQUIPMENT

A   B

Map Name/No

THE HIKE

Start Time

End Time

Actual Distance

Total No of Steps

Calories
Burned

M   P

POINTS OF INTEREST

Difficulty Level (1 Easy 5 Hard) △

Enjoyment Level (1 Bad 5 Good) ♡

Overall Grade (1 Bad 5 Good) ☆

Notes
Facilities
Parking
Costs
Nature
Etc

MY MUNRO TOTAL

THE PLAN

Date

MUNRO NAME

My Ref

Meet up time/ location

Area name/ Closest Town

Est. Duration

GPS / Latitude & Longitude / Grid Ref

Est. Distance

Km
Miles

Loop / Line & Back / One Way   Day Trip / Overnight/ Holiday

Local Contact

Accommodation Info

THE EQUIPMENT

A   B

Map Name/No

THE HIKE

Start Time

End Time

Actual Distance

Total No of Steps

Calories
Burned

POINTS OF INTEREST

Difficulty Level (1 Easy 5 Hard) △

Enjoyment Level (1 Bad 5 Good) ♡

Overall Grade (1 Bad 5 Good) ☆

Notes
Facilities
Parking
Costs
Nature
Etc

MY MUNRO TOTAL

THE PLAN

Date

MUNRO NAME

My Ref

Meet up time/ location	Area name/ Closest Town
Est. Duration	GPS / Latitude & Longitude / Grid Ref
Est. Distance Km Miles	Loop / Line & Back / One Way Day Trip / Overnight/ Holiday
Local Contact	Accommodation Info

THE EQUIPMENT

A B

Map Name/No

THE HIKE

(M) (P)

Start Time

End Time

Actual Distance

Total No of Steps

Calories Burned

POINTS OF INTEREST

Difficulty Level (1 Easy 5 Hard) △

Enjoyment Level (1 Bad 5 Good) ♡

Overall Grade (1 Bad 5 Good) ☆

Notes
Facilities
Parking
Costs
Nature
Etc

MY MUNRO TOTAL

THE PLAN

MUNRO NAME

My Ref

Date

Meet up time/ location

Area name/ Closest Town

Est. Duration

GPS / Latitude & Longitude / Grid Ref

Est. Distance

Km
Miles

Loop / Line & Back / One Way   Day Trip / Overnight/ Holiday

Local Contact

Accommodation Info

THE EQUIPMENT

A   B

Map Name/No

THE HIKE

M   P

Start Time

End Time

Actual Distance

Total No of Steps

Calories
Burned

POINTS OF INTEREST

Difficulty Level (1 Easy 5 Hard) △

Enjoyment Level (1 Bad 5 Good) ♡

Overall Grade (1 Bad 5 Good) ☆

Notes
Facilities
Parking
Costs
Nature
Etc

MY MUNRO TOTAL

THE PLAN

Date

MUNRO NAME

My Ref

Meet up time/ location

Area name/ Closest Town

Est. Duration

GPS / Latitude & Longitude / Grid Ref

Est. Distance

Km
Miles

Loop / Line & Back / One Way   Day Trip / Overnight/ Holiday

Local Contact

Accommodation Info

THE EQUIPMENT

A B

Map Name/No

THE HIKE

M   P

Start Time

End Time

Actual Distance

Total No of Steps

Calories
Burned

POINTS OF INTEREST

Difficulty Level (1 Easy 5 Hard) △

Enjoyment Level (1 Bad 5 Good) ♡

Overall Grade (1 Bad 5 Good) ☆

Notes
Facilities
Parking
Costs
Nature
Etc

MY MUNRO TOTAL

THE PLAN

MUNRO NAME	**My Ref**

Date

Meet up time/ location

Area name/ Closest Town

Est. Duration

GPS / Latitude & Longitude / Grid Ref

Est. Distance

Km
Miles

Loop / Line & Back / One Way   Day Trip / Overnight/ Holiday

Local Contact

Accommodation Info

THE EQUIPMENT

A   B

Map Name/No

THE HIKE

(M) (P)

Start Time

End Time

Actual Distance

Total No of Steps

Calories
Burned

POINTS OF INTEREST

Difficulty Level (1 Easy 5 Hard) △

Enjoyment Level (1 Bad 5 Good) ♡

Overall Grade (1 Bad 5 Good) ☆

Notes
Facilities
Parking
Costs
Nature
Etc

MY MUNRO TOTAL

THE PLAN

MUNRO NAME

My Ref

Date

Meet up time/ location

Area name/ Closest Town

Est. Duration

GPS / Latitude & Longitude / Grid Ref

Est. Distance

Km
Miles

Loop / Line & Back / One Way   Day Trip / Overnight/ Holiday

Local Contact

Accommodation Info

THE EQUIPMENT

A   B

Map Name/No

THE HIKE

Start Time

End Time

Actual Distance

Total No of Steps

Calories
Burned

(M) (P)

POINTS OF INTEREST

Difficulty Level (1 Easy 5 Hard) △

Enjoyment Level (1 Bad 5 Good) ♡

Overall Grade (1 Bad 5 Good) ☆

Notes
Facilities
Parking
Costs
Nature
Etc

MY MUNRO TOTAL

THE PLAN

MUNRO NAME

My Ref

Date

| Meet up time/ location | Area name/ Closest Town |

| Est. Duration | GPS / Latitude & Longitude / Grid Ref |

| Est. Distance | Km / Miles |

Loop / Line & Back / One Way   Day Trip / Overnight/ Holiday

| Local Contact | Accommodation Info |

THE EQUIPMENT

A   B

Map Name/No

THE HIKE

Start Time

End Time

Actual Distance

Total No of Steps

Calories Burned

POINTS OF INTEREST

Difficulty Level (1 Easy 5 Hard) △

Enjoyment Level (1 Bad 5 Good) ♡

Overall Grade (1 Bad 5 Good) ☆

Notes
Facilities
Parking
Costs
Nature
Etc

MY MUNRO TOTAL

THE PLAN

MUNRO NAME

My Ref

Date

Meet up time/ location

Area name/ Closest Town

Est. Duration

GPS / Latitude & Longitude / Grid Ref

Est. Distance

Km
Miles

Loop / Line & Back / One Way   Day Trip / Overnight/ Holiday

Local Contact

Accommodation Info

THE EQUIPMENT

A   B

Map Name/No

THE HIKE

Start Time

End Time

Actual Distance

(M)   (P)

Total No of Steps

Calories
Burned

POINTS OF INTEREST

Difficulty Level (1 Easy 5 Hard) △

Enjoyment Level (1 Bad 5 Good) ♡

Overall Grade (1 Bad 5 Good) ☆

Notes
Facilities
Parking
Costs
Nature
Etc

MY MUNRO TOTAL

THE PLAN

Date

MUNRO NAME		My Ref

Meet up time/ location

Area name/ Closest Town

Est. Duration

GPS / Latitude & Longitude / Grid Ref

Est. Distance

Km
Miles

Loop / Line & Back / One Way   Day Trip / Overnight/ Holiday

Local Contact

Accommodation Info

THE EQUIPMENT

A   B

Map Name/No

THE HIKE

Start Time

End Time

Actual Distance

Total No of Steps

Calories
Burned

(M) (P)

POINTS OF INTEREST

Difficulty Level (1 Easy 5 Hard) △

Enjoyment Level (1 Bad 5 Good) ♡

Overall Grade (1 Bad 5 Good) ☆

Notes
Facilities
Parking
Costs
Nature
Etc

MY MUNRO TOTAL

THE PLAN

Date

MUNRO NAME

My Ref

Meet up time/ location	Area name/ Closest Town
Est. Duration	GPS / Latitude & Longitude / Grid Ref
Est. Distance Km Miles	Loop / Line & Back / One Way Day Trip / Overnight/ Holiday
Local Contact	Accommodation Info

THE EQUIPMENT

A   B

Map Name/No

THE HIKE

(M) (P)

Start Time

End Time

Actual Distance

Total No of Steps

Calories Burned

POINTS OF INTEREST

Difficulty Level (1 Easy 5 Hard) △

Enjoyment Level (1 Bad 5 Good) ♡

Overall Grade (1 Bad 5 Good) ☆

Notes
Facilities
Parking
Costs
Nature
Etc

MY MUNRO TOTAL

THE PLAN

Date	MUNRO NAME	My Ref

Meet up time/ location | Area name/ Closest Town

Est. Duration | GPS / Latitude & Longitude / Grid Ref

Est. Distance _____ Km Miles

Loop / Line & Back / One Way   Day Trip / Overnight/ Holiday

Local Contact | Accommodation Info

THE EQUIPMENT

A B

Map Name/No

THE HIKE

Start Time

End Time

Actual Distance

Total No of Steps

(M) (P)

POINTS OF INTEREST

Calories Burned

Difficulty Level (1 Easy 5 Hard) △

Enjoyment Level (1 Bad 5 Good) ♡

Overall Grade (1 Bad 5 Good) ☆

Notes
Facilities
Parking
Costs
Nature
Etc

MY MUNRO TOTAL

THE PLAN

MUNRO NAME

My Ref

Date

Meet up time/ location

Area name/ Closest Town

Est. Duration

GPS / Latitude & Longitude / Grid Ref

Est. Distance   Km
                       Miles

Loop / Line & Back / One Way   Day Trip / Overnight/ Holiday

Local Contact

Accommodation Info

THE EQUIPMENT

A   B

Map Name/No

THE HIKE

(M)   (P)

Start Time

End Time

Actual Distance

Total No of Steps

Calories
Burned

POINTS OF INTEREST

Difficulty Level (1 Easy 5 Hard) △

Enjoyment Level (1 Bad 5 Good) ♡

Overall Grade (1 Bad 5 Good) ☆

Notes
Facilities
Parking
Costs
Nature
Etc

MY MUNRO TOTAL

THE PLAN

Date

MUNRO NAME		My Ref

Meet up time/ location

Area name/ Closest Town

Est. Duration

GPS / Latitude & Longitude / Grid Ref

Est. Distance   Km
                       Miles

Loop / Line & Back / One Way   Day Trip / Overnight/ Holiday

Local Contact

Accommodation Info

THE EQUIPMENT

A   B

Map Name/No

THE HIKE

M   P

Start Time

End Time

Actual Distance

Total No of Steps

Calories Burned

POINTS OF INTEREST

Difficulty Level (1 Easy 5 Hard)

Enjoyment Level (1 Bad 5 Good)

Overall Grade (1 Bad 5 Good)

Notes
Facilities
Parking
Costs
Nature
Etc

MY MUNRO TOTAL

THE PLAN

Date

MUNRO NAME

My Ref

| Meet up time/ location | Area name/ Closest Town |

| Est. Duration | GPS / Latitude & Longitude / Grid Ref |

| Est. Distance | Km Miles |

Loop / Line & Back / One Way   Day Trip / Overnight/ Holiday

| Local Contact | Accommodation Info |

THE EQUIPMENT

A   B

Map Name/No

THE HIKE

(M) (P)

Start Time

End Time

Actual Distance

Total No of Steps

Calories Burned

POINTS OF INTEREST

Difficulty Level (1 Easy 5 Hard) △

Enjoyment Level (1 Bad 5 Good) ♡

Overall Grade (1 Bad 5 Good) ☆

Notes
Facilities
Parking
Costs
Nature
Etc

MY MUNRO TOTAL

THE PLAN

MUNRO NAME

My Ref

Date

Meet up time/ location

Area name/ Closest Town

Est. Duration

GPS / Latitude & Longitude / Grid Ref

Est. Distance

Km
Miles

Local Contact

Loop / Line & Back / One Way   Day Trip / Overnight/ Holiday

Accommodation Info

THE EQUIPMENT

A   B

Map Name/No

THE HIKE

Start Time

End Time

Actual Distance

M   P

Total No of Steps

Calories
Burned

POINTS OF INTEREST

Difficulty Level (1 Easy 5 Hard)

Enjoyment Level (1 Bad 5 Good)

Overall Grade (1 Bad 5 Good)

Notes
Facilities
Parking
Costs
Nature
Etc

MY MUNRO TOTAL

THE PLAN

	MUNRO NAME	My Ref
Date		

Meet up time/ location

Area name/ Closest Town

Est. Duration

GPS / Latitude & Longitude / Grid Ref

Est. Distance   Km
Miles

Loop / Line & Back / One Way   Day Trip / Overnight/ Holiday

Local Contact

Accommodation Info

THE EQUIPMENT

A B

Map Name/No

THE HIKE

(M) (P)

Start Time

End Time

Actual Distance

Total No of Steps

Calories
Burned

POINTS OF INTEREST

Difficulty Level (1 Easy 5 Hard) △

Enjoyment Level (1 Bad 5 Good) ♡

Overall Grade (1 Bad 5 Good) ☆

Notes
Facilities
Parking
Costs
Nature
Etc

MY MUNRO TOTAL

THE PLAN

	MUNRO NAME	My Ref
Date		

Meet up time/ location

Area name/ Closest Town

Est. Duration

GPS / Latitude & Longitude / Grid Ref

Est. Distance

Km
Miles

Loop / Line & Back / One Way   Day Trip / Overnight/ Holiday

Local Contact

Accommodation Info

THE EQUIPMENT

A   B

Map Name/No

THE HIKE

(M)   (P)

Start Time

End Time

Actual Distance

Total No of Steps

Calories
Burned

POINTS OF INTEREST

Difficulty Level (1 Easy 5 Hard) △

Enjoyment Level (1 Bad 5 Good) ♡

Overall Grade (1 Bad 5 Good) ☆

Notes
Facilities
Parking
Costs
Nature
Etc

MY MUNRO TOTAL

THE PLAN

MUNRO NAME

My Ref

Date

Meet up time/ location

Area name/ Closest Town

Est. Duration

GPS / Latitude & Longitude / Grid Ref

Est. Distance   Km
                       Miles

Loop / Line & Back / One Way   Day Trip / Overnight/ Holiday

Local Contact

Accommodation Info

THE EQUIPMENT

A   B

Map Name/No

THE HIKE

Start Time

End Time

Actual Distance

(M) (P)

Total No of Steps

Calories
Burned

POINTS OF INTEREST

Difficulty Level (1 Easy 5 Hard) △

Enjoyment Level (1 Bad 5 Good) ♡

Overall Grade (1 Bad 5 Good) ☆

Notes
Facilities
Parking
Costs
Nature
Etc

MY MUNRO TOTAL

THE PLAN

Date

MUNRO NAME		My Ref

Meet up time/ location

Area name/ Closest Town

Est. Duration

GPS / Latitude & Longitude / Grid Ref

Est. Distance   Km / Miles

Loop / Line & Back / One Way   Day Trip / Overnight/ Holiday

Local Contact

Accommodation Info

THE EQUIPMENT

A   B

Map Name/No

THE HIKE

M   P

Start Time

End Time

Actual Distance

Total No of Steps

POINTS OF INTEREST

Calories Burned

Difficulty Level (1 Easy 5 Hard) △

Enjoyment Level (1 Bad 5 Good) ♡

Overall Grade (1 Bad 5 Good) ☆

Notes
Facilities
Parking
Costs
Nature
Etc

MY MUNRO TOTAL

THE PLAN

Date

MUNRO NAME

My Ref

Meet up time/ location

Area name/ Closest Town

Est. Duration

GPS / Latitude & Longitude / Grid Ref

Est. Distance

Km
Miles

Loop / Line & Back / One Way   Day Trip / Overnight/ Holiday

Local Contact

Accommodation Info

THE EQUIPMENT

A B

Map Name/No

THE HIKE

Start Time

End Time

Actual Distance

Total No of Steps

(M) (P)

POINTS OF INTEREST

Calories
Burned

Difficulty Level (1 Easy 5 Hard) △

Enjoyment Level (1 Bad 5 Good) ♡

Overall Grade (1 Bad 5 Good) ☆

Notes
Facilities
Parking
Costs
Nature
Etc

MY MUNRO TOTAL

THE PLAN

Date	**MUNRO NAME** ___ **My Ref** ___
Meet up time/ location	Area name/ Closest Town
Est. Duration	GPS / Latitude & Longitude / Grid Ref
Est. Distance _____ Km Miles	
	Loop / Line & Back / One Way Day Trip / Overnight/ Holiday
Local Contact	Accommodation Info

THE EQUIPMENT

A B

Map Name/No

THE HIKE

Start Time

End Time

Actual Distance

(M) (P)

Total No of Steps

Calories Burned

POINTS OF INTEREST

Difficulty Level (1 Easy 5 Hard) △

Enjoyment Level (1 Bad 5 Good) ♡

Overall Grade (1 Bad 5 Good) ☆

Notes
Facilities
Parking
Costs
Nature
Etc

MY MUNRO TOTAL

THE PLAN

Date

MUNRO NAME

My Ref

Meet up time/ location

Area name/ Closest Town

Est. Duration

GPS / Latitude & Longitude / Grid Ref

Est. Distance

Km
Miles

Loop / Line & Back / One Way   Day Trip / Overnight/ Holiday

Local Contact

Accommodation Info

THE EQUIPMENT

A   B

Map Name/No

THE HIKE

Start Time

End Time

Actual Distance

M   P

Total No of Steps

Calories
Burned

POINTS OF INTEREST

Difficulty Level (1 Easy 5 Hard) △

Enjoyment Level (1 Bad 5 Good) ♡

Overall Grade (1 Bad 5 Good) ☆

Notes
Facilities
Parking
Costs
Nature
Etc

MY MUNRO TOTAL

THE PLAN

Date

MUNRO NAME

My Ref

Meet up time/ location	Area name/ Closest Town

Est. Duration	GPS / Latitude & Longitude / Grid Ref

Est. Distance

Km
Miles

Loop / Line & Back / One Way   Day Trip / Overnight/ Holiday

Local Contact	Accommodation Info

THE EQUIPMENT

A   B

Map Name/No

THE HIKE

(M) (P)

Start Time

End Time

Actual Distance

Total No of Steps

Calories
Burned

POINTS OF INTEREST

Difficulty Level (1 Easy 5 Hard)

Enjoyment Level (1 Bad 5 Good)

Overall Grade (1 Bad 5 Good)

Notes
Facilities
Parking
Costs
Nature
Etc

MY MUNRO TOTAL

THE PLAN

MUNRO NAME

My Ref

Date

Meet up time/ location

Area name/ Closest Town

Est. Duration

GPS / Latitude & Longitude / Grid Ref

Est. Distance

Km
Miles

Loop / Line & Back / One Way   Day Trip / Overnight/ Holiday

Local Contact

Accommodation Info

THE EQUIPMENT

A   B

Map Name/No

THE HIKE

Start Time

End Time

M   P

Actual Distance

Total No of Steps

Calories
Burned

POINTS OF INTEREST

Difficulty Level (1 Easy 5 Hard) △

Enjoyment Level (1 Bad 5 Good) ♡

Overall Grade (1 Bad 5 Good) ☆

Notes
Facilities
Parking
Costs
Nature
Etc

MY MUNRO TOTAL

THE PLAN

Date

	MUNRO NAME	My Ref

Meet up time/ location

Est. Duration

Est. Distance   Km Miles

Local Contact

Area name/ Closest Town

GPS / Latitude & Longitude / Grid Ref

Loop / Line & Back / One Way   Day Trip / Overnight/ Holiday

Accommodation Info

THE EQUIPMENT

A B

Map Name/No

THE HIKE

M   P

Start Time

End Time

Actual Distance

Total No of Steps

Calories Burned

POINTS OF INTEREST

Difficulty Level (1 Easy 5 Hard)

Enjoyment Level (1 Bad 5 Good)

Overall Grade (1 Bad 5 Good)

Notes
Facilities
Parking
Costs
Nature
Etc

MY MUNRO TOTAL

THE PLAN

	MUNRO NAME	My Ref
Date		

Meet up time/ location	Area name/ Closest Town
Est. Duration	GPS / Latitude & Longitude / Grid Ref
Est. Distance Km Miles	
	Loop / Line & Back / One Way Day Trip / Overnight/ Holiday
Local Contact	Accommodation Info

THE EQUIPMENT

A B

Map Name/No

THE HIKE

(M) (P)

Start Time

End Time

Actual Distance

Total No of Steps

Calories
Burned

POINTS OF INTEREST

Difficulty Level (1 Easy 5 Hard) △

Enjoyment Level (1 Bad 5 Good) ♡

Overall Grade (1 Bad 5 Good) ☆

Notes
Facilities
Parking
Costs
Nature
Etc

MY MUNRO TOTAL

NOTES

NOTES

NOTES

ESSENTIAL KIT

This of course is dependant on the remoteness and difficulty of your hike.
But it is always useful to remind yourself and to stay safe.

1 Map & Compass, Pen Knife ☐

2 Walking Shoes / Boots & spare Dry socks ☐

3 Enough Food & Water ☐

4 (Reserve) Waterproof Clothing & Warm Hat ☐

5 First Aid Kit / Basic Repair Kit ☐

6 Sunscreen, Sun Glasses ☐

7 Fully Charged Mobile Phone / Battery Reserve ☐

8 Torch & Matches/ Lighter ☐

9 Camera Equipt, Battery solutions ☐

10 This Journal & Pen ☐

WALKING / HIKING PLAN

Event / Route   Date

1 Choose Location & Route (Check Reviews) ☐

2 Research Conditions, Weather etc ☐

3 Plan Route, Stops & Timings ☐

4 Travel Planning:How to get there & back ☐

5 Check RainFall, Sunrise & Sunset Times ☐

6 Research terrain - correct footwear ☐

7 Food & Water Requirements (refill stops etc) ☐

8 Make Equipment Packing List ☐

9 Camera Equipt, Battery solutions, Safety ☐

10 Location 'Extras': Research-
     (Points of interest,Features, Wildlife etc) ☐

Printed in Great Britain
by Amazon

34666695R00185